Inventors
and
Inventions

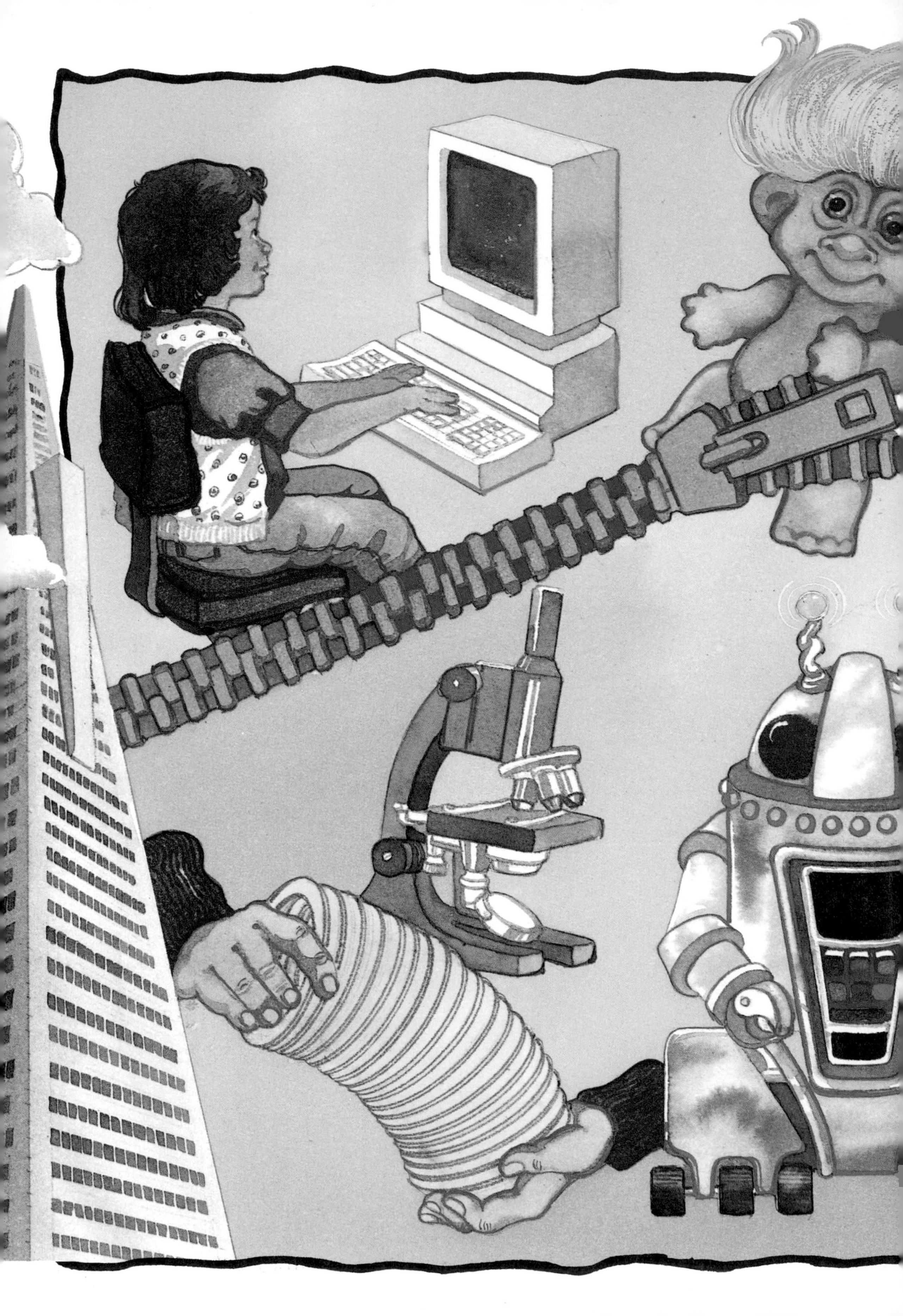

Inventors and Inventions

A Supplement to Childcraft—The How and Why Library

World Book, Inc.
a Scott Fetzer company
Chicago London Sydney Toronto

World Book, Inc.
525 W. Monroe
Chicago, IL 60661

ISBN 0-7166-0693-3
Library of Congress Catalog Card No. 65-25105

Printed in the United States of America

a/ic

The publisher gratefully acknowledges the courtesy of the following companies for permission to use illustrations of their products on the cover of this book:

Russ Berrie (Troll)
James Industries Inc. (Slinky®)

Editorial Advisory Board
for Childcraft—The How and Why Library

Staff

Preface

Would you like to invent a different kind of bicycle? What about a new game or a special way of getting your homework done? Inventions begin with ideas, and if you've ever sketched a wonderful machine you've thought up, or ever had an idea about doing something in a way that's better than the way it's done now, you have an inventive mind. This book tells about other people with inventive minds and the inventions they have made.

First, you'll learn about the "inventive process"—that is, the way inventors get ideas and turn them into useful products. Then you'll read about all kinds of inventions, from inventions that have changed the world to inventions that are just for fun. While you're reading, you may come up with some ideas of your own. You even may want to try some of them out. Who knows? One of your ideas may grow into a real invention someday.

Contents

How Inventions Happen 8

Inventions for Fun 42

Everyday Inventions 74

Inventions That Changed the World 102

Inventions for Safety   130

Inventions for Learning   160

Inventing A New World   184

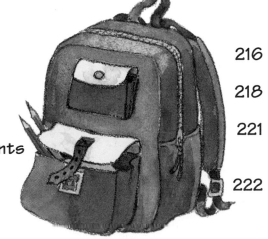

HAPPEN

CLOUD

COLOR

"If only . . ." Inventors may begin more daydreams with these two words than any others. "If only I could fly like a bird." "If only I could build a building hundreds of feet high." Inventors don't stop at dreaming, though. They get to work.

First of all, inventors think and think. When they get an idea, they write it down. They read and learn. They do experiments. Sometimes they succeed. Other times they fail. But they never give up. After all this, with a lot of patience and a little luck, a new invention may be born.

DREAMING of WINGS

Hello there! A legendary "flying machine" is talking to you. I'm a barn swallow. Every year, we fly thousands of miles between our summer and winter homes. Throughout history, people have looked up at us, wishing they too could fly.

This dream has inspired many people to invent ways to leave the ground. In 1783, two brave Frenchmen became the first people to fly. They knew that hot air rises. So they climbed into a basket fastened to a large balloon. They used a fire in an iron pot to heat the air inside the balloon. The balloon rose at least 300 feet (91 meters).

Balloons fell short of these early fliers' dreams, though. Balloons drifted with the wind and did not go where the pilots wanted. They wanted to have more control over their flights. So inventors started looking at us birds as a model for a brand new kind of flying machine.

Look at my wings. See how they're curved? Air passes more swiftly over these curved wings than under them. Slow-moving air has a higher pressure than fast-moving air. So this high pressure beneath my wings forces my body up. This force is called *lift*. Lift is what keeps a bird—and an airplane—up in the air.

In 1799, Sir George Cayley, a British engineer, built a small aircraft with curved wings. It was called a *glider* because it glided on the air. Another inventor, a

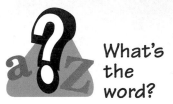

What's the word?

Engineers design all kinds of things, including roads, machines, buildings, bridges, and products we use every day. The word *engineer* comes from the Latin word *ingeniare*, which means "to design" or "to create."

German engineer named Otto Lilienthal, devoted years to perfecting a glider. Lilienthal piloted his craft by swinging his body from side to side as he hung from its large, lightweight wings.

Meanwhile, Octave Chanute, an American engineer, heard about the experiments that Lilienthal was doing. Chanute developed a double-winged glider—or *biplane*—that several pilots flew successfully.

Naturally, we swallows watched all these goings-on. And I guess people were still watching us make our long journeys. Because they kept on trying to invent a long-distance flying machine.

In 1900, people's dreams of flight really started to take off. Two bicycle makers, Wilbur Wright and his brother Orville,

began testing a glider near Kitty Hawk, North Carolina. Before long, the Wrights worked out a way to control their glider in flight.

Then the brothers turned their attention to building a powered glider— an airplane. They tried out different wing shapes. They also discovered that propellers added lift by acting like spinning wings. To turn the propellers, they designed a lightweight gasoline motor. Finally, they finished their plane, named *Flyer*.

In December 1903, the Wrights hauled *Flyer* to Kitty Hawk. There they laid sixty feet (18 meters) of track and placed a wheeled platform on it. Then they set *Flyer* on the platform.

Orville stretched out on *Flyer*'s lower wing. With its propellers whirring, *Flyer* rolled along the track. The plane picked up speed and then lifted about ten feet (3 meters) into the air. For the first time, a heavier-than-air machine flew under its own power. The dream of flight had come true!

With helicopters, supersonic jets, and even space shuttles, flying machines have come a long way. But in my opinion, we birds are still the best "flying machines." How would you like to *really* fly like a bird—perching in trees and alighting on rooftops, flitting here and there as easy as you ride your bike? Maybe someday you'll invent a way to do that. Just put on your inventor's cap. And keep dreaming!

YOU CAN DO IT!

Build a model glider

Things you need:

- ✔ Styrofoam dinner plate
- ✔ marker
- ✔ scissors
- ✔ ruler
- ✔ 1 small paper clip

4"

1½"

1. Cut a 4-inch (10-cm) square from the plate.
2. Cut out a large triangle from the square with one side of the square as the base. This triangle is the glider's body and wings. Keep one of the smaller triangles for a rudder.
3. Draw a dot in the middle of the base of the wing. Cut a slot from the dot halfway up the triangle.
4. One-fourth of the way up the longest side of the rudder, cut a slot about 1-1/2 inches (3.75 cm) deep.
5. Cut off the tip of the rudder at an angle and fit the slot on the rudder into the slot on the wing.
6. Slide a paper clip onto the nose of the glider.

Try flying the glider upside down. What happens? Also experiment with different shapes for the glider's body and rudder. Which shapes fly best?

What's the word?

Harebrained means just what it says—having the brain of a hare. Translate that to mean "silly" or "foolish." Whoever made up the word hundreds of years ago certainly didn't put those rabbit cousins, hares, into the same class as the wise owl or noble lion.

Harebrained Ideas?

Almost every invention starts out as a "harebrained idea." Before a new invention catches on, people often laugh at it. Perhaps they laugh because they don't understand the idea or they can't imagine any use for the invention. Often, the laughers are right. But a few harebrained ideas have been destined for greatness.

One invention apparently not destined for greatness was invented in 1840 in England. It was a tall, inflated hat that was supposed to keep a wearer who fell into deep water afloat.

Harebrained inventors have not stopped at hats, though. Cecil Slemp "improved" a pair of men's shoes in 1974. He reversed the toe and heel on the sole of the shoe. The footprints of the wearer would then appear to be going in the opposite direction and confuse anyone who might be tracking him.

Women's shoes have been "improved," too. In 1960, Mart Irving and William Duncan invented high heels with lights that flickered on and off as the wearer walked.

Some inventors have concentrated on inventions for animals rather than for people. A. Jackson made bird-sized eyeglasses in 1903 to protect chickens' eyes from pecking by other chickens.

Can you imagine a horse with an umbrella? Sarah Ruth could. She patented two umbrellalike shades in 1868 to keep horses comfortable in the sun.

What's the word?

A **patent** is a government paper that gives an inventor the right to be the only person who can make or sell an invention for a certain number of years. A patent helps an inventor prevent other people from copying the invention and making money from it.

Bright idea

You probably have seen ads for the latest inventions that slice, dice, chop, and peel. However, multipurpose kitchen gadgets are not new. Almost one hundred years ago, R. M. Gardiner patented a gadget that not only stored, sliced, and grated food but could also be used as a trap for mice and flies!

Alarms make up another class of nutty inventions. Patented alarms include security systems like Thomas Burghart's car alarm of 1921. In addition to sounding loudly when someone tried to steal the car, it triggered cuffs that shot out from under the driver's seat and grabbed the ankles of the thief.

Needless to say, these products did not make their inventors rich or famous. But a word to the wise: Think twice before you laugh at a harebrained idea. Many brave inventors who kept trying while other

people laughed at them ended up enjoying the last laugh.

Take Chester Carlson, for example. Not a soul was interested in his copying machine back in the 1930's. After getting a patent for his idea, he needed money to build the machine. He approached several large companies. "No, thanks," they all said. After more than five years of hard work and money problems, a small company finally invested in Carlson's invention. What did he invent? Perhaps you've heard of it. It's called the Xerox machine.

Then there was John Holland. All his life he had dreamed about an underwater boat. In 1875, he offered his plan to the U.S. Navy. The Navy turned him down. But when Holland showed off his boat—the submarine—25 years later, the Navy was the first in line to buy several of them.

George Ferris, Jr., too, was teased for his "dizzy" idea. Organizers of a major world's fair to be held in Chicago in 1893 announced their need for a main attraction. Ferris responded by telling the organizers of his plan to build a steel wheel 250 feet (76 meters) in diameter from which 36

Who did it?

passenger cars would hang. The wheel would spin, giving people the ride of their life. As Ferris set out to build his big wheel, though, people called his project "G. W.'s cockeyed dream." But on June 21, 1893, the enormous structure began to turn. And people loved it! Ferris' invention was the model for today's Ferris wheel.

How about you? Do you have any "harebrained" ideas? Invite your friends to think up wacky inventions with you. Who knows? Your ideas may be worth a fortune. Then you can laugh all the way to the bank.

Rain (**A**) goes through hose (**B**) and waters small palm (**C**)–Palm grows and tickles dog (**D**), causing him to laugh and get dignified old owl (**E**) very sore–Owl throws rock (**F**) at dog, misses him and breaks string (**G**), releasing spring (**H**) and causing ping pong racket (**I**) to swat acrobatic manikin (**J**) to swing around many times and rotate brush (**K**). At times, this device might prove slightly inconvenient because you have to wait for rain.

Rube Goldberg (1883-1970)

Rube Goldberg takes the prize for the all-time nuttiest inventor. But Rube never applied for a patent because his inventions were in his comic strips. Rube's first cartoons appeared in the sports section of the *San Francisco Chronicle*. In time, other newspapers began to print them as well.

One of Rube's most popular strips featured Professor Lucifer Butts. The professor dreamed up inventions that made the simplest tasks hilariously complicated. The back scrubber is a good example.

Earle Dickson, A Cut Above

There's an old saying that goes, "Necessity is the mother of invention." In other words, people invent things to fill needs or solve problems they have. Mix imagination with this necessity, and you may end up with a great invention. Earle Dickson did just that in 1920.

While learning to cook, Earle's new wife, Josephine, often cut or burned herself in the kitchen. Luckily, Earle worked for Johnson & Johnson, a company that made tape and gauze (gawz) used by doctors. Of course, they had a lot of this around the house. So whenever Josephine hurt herself, her loving husband taped gauze to her wound.

Earle treated his wife a number of times, only to have the bandage fall off. He became determined to design a ready-to-use bandage that would stay in place and stay clean. That was the need. Now, the imagination comes in.

Earle and Josephine (on the left side of the photograph) pose with the actors who starred in a play about them, *left*.

An assortment of Band-Aid® packages from the past, *above*.

Earle thought it over and had a great idea—he would make tape-and-gauze strips ahead of time. He stuck gauze pads in the middle of pieces of tape. But it occurred to him that the gauze would not be germ-free if left in the open. And the sticky side of the tape would soon dry up.

Add a little more imagination.

Earle decided to try using a material called *crinoline* (KRIHN uh lihn) to cover the sticky side of the tape. It worked. It was easy to remove, and as an added bonus, Josephine could even apply the bandage herself.

The next time Josephine cut herself, she peeled the ready-made bandage from the crinoline and applied it to her wound. She beamed. Her husband was a genius.

A person Earle worked with convinced him to show his idea to the bosses at Johnson & Johnson. They liked it. Someone else came up with a name for Earle's ingenious product, which was a new *aid* in *bandaging*. That's why today these handy strips are called Band-Aid® Brand Adhesive Bandages.

"And I'd Like to Thank . . ."

It thrusts up from the ground, gleaming glass and steel. Standing at its base, you can't see the top unless you lean waaaaaay back. Clouds hide its top on rainy days. Thousands of people work and live inside—it's a skyscraper. William Le Baron Jenney designed the first skyscraper in the late 1800's. Many inventions were necessary to make it possible. Let's listen in as Jenney tells about them. . . .

Presenter: And the award for the inventor who contributed most to changing the face of American cities goes to William Le Baron Jenney for his design of the first metal-frame skyscraper. (Applause)

Mr. Jenney: Thank you for this award. But I do not deserve all the credit. My success rests on the earlier efforts of many other inventors. I never would have been able to design my skyscraper if certain inventions hadn't been available already.

For example, before my design, many tall buildings were constructed with thick brick-and-stone walls at the base. These walls supported almost all the weight of the upper floors. If a building rose more than five or six stories, the walls at the base had to be very thick.

These kinds of walls cost a lot of money and labor. I wanted to do my building differently, and I finally figured out how. Think of a bird cage. It is made only of thin metal columns, but you could put a heavy item on top of it, and it would not bend. In the same way, I thought, maybe a "cage" of strong beams could hold up a building. Luckily for me, the ideal material for building my metal frame—rolled steel columns—had just come onto the market. They were lighter and stronger than iron, which was more commonly used in my day. Finally, I was on my way!

Now that I had figured out a way to make tall buildings with metal frames, there were lots of window possibilities—wide windows, tall windows, just plain big windows. Imagine a skyscraper with windows the size of those on ordinary

Who did it?

It's hard to picture a building today without light bulbs. American Thomas Alva Edison invented the modern light bulb in 1879. But many others worked on light bulbs before him. In fact, British inventor Joseph Wilson Swan also unveiled a light bulb in 1879. Edison didn't stop with light bulbs, though. His 1,093 patents included lamp sockets, electricity meters, and safety fuses, all of which made electric lights practical.

buildings. It would look funny—and be dark and drab inside, too. So I'd like to thank the French glassmakers who developed plate glass windows in the late 1600's.

These glassmakers poured the liquid glass mixture into big, flat molds, called *casting tables*. Then they heated the glass in ovens to strengthen it. This method produced large, strong windows—ideal for the walls of a skyscraper.

Now it was possible to have a beautiful, towering building. But there's no sense in building a skyscraper so tall that it would take an hour to climb the stairs to the top! So tonight I'd like to give special thanks to Elisha Graves Otis, the inventor of the safety elevator.

Most early elevators carried freight but not people. This was because old-fashioned elevators were very dangerous. They dangled at the end of a rope. If the rope broke, the elevator crashed to the ground.

In 1854, Otis, a factory worker, demonstrated his safety elevator. He attached a track of jagged metal teeth to the sides of an elevator shaft. Otis's elevator still hung from a rope, but when the rope was cut, latches on the sides of the elevator caught on the metal track and stopped the elevator's fall. Now people in buildings like mine ride between the floors without fearing for their lives.

And finally, I'd like to thank all of you for your recognition.

Presenter: Well, Mr. Jenney, you've been very generous with your thanks. You've shown us that advances as important as yours depend on the work of many inventors who came before. I'm sure many of these inventors would be amazed at how their inventions would one day be used. So let's hear it, folks, for Mr. William Le Baron Jenney, inventor of the modern skyscraper, and all the other inventors that made his success possible!

When and where

After Jenney finished his Home Insurance Building in Chicago in 1885, Chicago became the testing ground for new ideas in skyscrapers. Why Chicago? Because about 17,500 buildings burned down in the Great Chicago Fire of 1871. While rebuilding Chicago, architects and engineers seized the chance to try out ideas for creating a truly modern looking city. In 1888, a Chicago newspaper became one of the first to use the word *skyscraper* in print.

Stuck on Stickies

Here is the story of an adhesive that doesn't stay stuck, and how its discovery led to one of the most popular inventions on desks in schools and offices everywhere. Maybe a few are clinging to the telephone, the refrigerator, or one of your homework assignments. Maybe you've used them at school to send messages to your friends during quiet time, or post ideas on the blackboard.

In the 1960's, a scientist named Spencer Silver was experimenting with different kinds of adhesives. He worked for Minnesota Mining and Manufacturing Company, known as 3M. It was his job to invent special adhesives that 3M could develop into new products.

One day, to Silver's surprise, he mixed together some ingredients and came up with a gooey, liquidy adhesive that behaved differently from most other adhesives. It wasn't very sticky! Silver's adhesive stuck two pieces of paper together well enough, but it peeled off easily instead of holding them firmly together. Some of the adhesive would stick to one sheet of paper, and some would stick to the other.

What's the word?

Scientists observe carefully and make experiments to find out about how things work. There are many branches of science, which comes from the Latin word for "knowledge"—*scientia*.

An **adhesive** is anything people use to stick other things together. Adhesives can be made from sticky tree sap or from artificial ingredients, such as nylon or plastics.

Silver was excited about his discovery, but he had no idea what to use the semi-sticky adhesive for. So he showed the stuff to anyone in the company who would look. All agreed that Silver's invention was nifty. But nobody would give him support to go further. "There's just no use for it," he was told again and again.

The big break for Silver's adhesive came in 1974 when another scientist at the company named Arthur Fry had a bright idea—at church! Fry sang in the choir. To help himself remember which songs the choir would sing, Fry liked to mark the

pages of his song book with little slips of
paper. If he put the book down, though,
or flipped the pages quickly, all the slips
of paper would fall out. Fry knew about
Silver's special adhesive. "What if we put
some on my bookmarks?" he thought.
"Then they wouldn't slip out."

After this, it didn't take much thought
for Fry to realize that he had discovered
a purpose for the gently sticky adhesive—
sticky note paper. People could stick this
note paper directly to other pieces of
paper, such as book pages and reports.
They wouldn't have to use paper clips,
staples, or tape. When people were done

with the notes, they could remove them easily.

Fry put together a team to figure out ways to make his idea into a useful product. For the idea to work, the adhesive had to "want" to stick permanently to the note paper. But then it had to willingly let go of whatever the note paper was stuck to. The team soon found a way to treat the note paper so that the adhesive stuck permanently to it.

Then Fry and his team had to invent a machine to produce the sticky notepads. Fry first built the machine in his own basement and later moved it to the factory.

Bright idea

Where do inventive ideas come from? Sometimes they come out of the dark. That happened with Becky Schroeder's Glo-Sheets.

"Wouldn't it be neat," ten-year-old Becky thought, "if there was some way to write in the dark? Maybe there's some way to 'light up' writing paper."

Becky began experimenting with phosphorescent (FAHS fuh REHS sent) materials, which give off light but not heat. Then she covered an acrylic (uh KRIHL ihk) board with phosphorescent paint. Acrylic is an especially tough plastic. After Becky exposed the board to light, the paint glowed through one or two sheets of paper in the dark.

Becky patented her invention when she was only twelve. Luckily, her father was a patent lawyer! All together, she got twelve

The new machine applied the adhesive to rolls of yellow paper, cut the paper into little squares and rectangles, and made them into pads.

These sticky notes were one of the most successful products the company had ever made. Before long, sticky notes were in offices all over the country. Later, people got stuck on sticky notes at home and school.

So next time you see a little colored piece of paper on the class calendar reminding everyone it's your birthday, think of Spencer Silver and Arthur Fry and the adhesive that didn't stick.

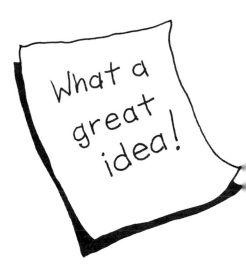

patents for Glo-Sheets and improvements on them.

By 1983, Becky was twenty-two and had started a company to market her Glo-Sheets. Doctors have used Glo-Sheets so they can read medical charts or take notes in dim hospital rooms without disturbing their patients. Becky has also sold Glo-Sheets to police departments and the United States Navy.

Leonardo's Crystal Ball

Leonardo da Vinci was a gifted inventor as well as a great artist. But he completed few of his inventions. Most he never even started to build. How do we know about Leonardo's ideas? Because he recorded much of what he saw and thought in his notebooks.

Leonardo's backward writing

Some of his notebooks were as large as wall posters, and others were small enough to carry on his belt. Many have not survived, but those that have are filled with drawings and lines of neat print. Leonardo wrote from right to left in his notebooks. Most people would have to hold the writing up to a mirror to read it. Why did Leonardo write "backward?" Perhaps he wanted to discourage nosy people from reading his notes!

The notebooks show Leonardo's ideas as well as the traits that made him great. Curiosity sums up his main strength as an inventor. He wanted to know how things worked. His desire for knowledge did not stop at machines but included flowing water, budding trees, flying birds, and human bodies. He also wondered how he could make things better. Another trait that made Leonardo great was his keen

What's the word?

In Leonardo's time, people did not have last names as we know them today. Instead they called themselves with the names of their fathers or hometowns. **Leonardo da Vinci** means "Leonard of Vinci" in English. The next time you read about Europeans who lived between 1400 and 1700, notice the *da*'s and *de*'s in their names. They mean "of" in Italian and French.

Who did it?

Leonardo da Vinci was not the only inventor who was also an artist. Samuel B. Morse, the inventor of the telegraph, painted portraits of Eli Whitney, the inventor of the cotton gin, and others.

eye. He observed the tiniest detail—the muscle in a horse's jaw, a flower petal, the light on a baby's curl.

Leonardo was born in 1452 on his father's country estate near the town of Vinci in Italy. It was there, perhaps, that he learned to observe and copy nature. Like many children, he may have kept lizards, crickets, snakes, butterflies, and grasshoppers as pets.

When Leonardo and his father moved to the city of Florence, Leonardo was sent

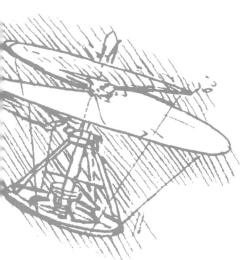

to the workshop of Andrea del Verrocchio (vuh ROH kee OH), a well known painter and sculptor.

In Verrocchio's workshop, Leonardo learned much of the *technology* known in his day. Technology means ways of getting work done. A painter had to know how to mix colors, known as *pigments,* for paints. Sculptors needed to know about metalworking because figures were made out of metal. Leonardo was interested in everything, well beyond his art! He jotted down what he learned from reading. He noted what he heard from the great people around him—popes, rulers, and other artists.

However, Leonardo improved most of the ideas that he borrowed until the

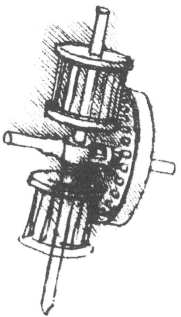

Leonardo's plan for a parachute

pictures in his notebooks looked like totally new ideas. In many cases, the pictures look like a vision of a future world—the world we know today.

Leonardo's notebooks include a drawing of a person with a parachute. Almost 300 years later, in 1783, a Frenchman named Sebastian Lenormand became the first person to float to earth with a parachute.

His sketches of a "flying machine" came well before any gliders or hot air balloons took to the skies.

Recently, a picture of a bicycle was found on the back of a page from one of Leonardo's notebooks. In the picture, a chain connected the rear wheel and the pedals. Experts guess it was drawn in the 1490's. Around the same time, Leonardo drew designs of a chain link like that used in modern bicycles. Although the first bicycle appeared in 1839, chain links were not used on bikes until nearly forty years later.

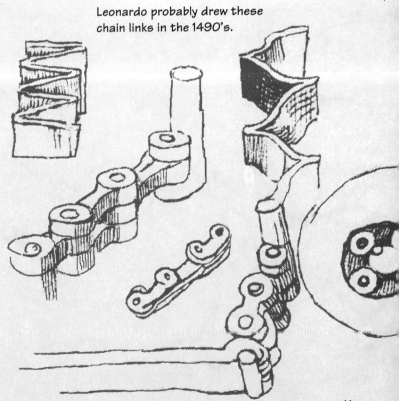

Leonardo probably drew these chain links in the 1490's.

Running, jumping, swinging,

throwing, building, pretending—the list of fun things to do goes on and on. It may surprise you to learn that toys have inventors just like cars, light bulbs, telescopes, and other "serious" things. Many inventors of toys and other forms of fun set out to improve a toy or make up a new game. In this chapter, you'll read about what a Danish toymaker invented as he was working on toy bricks.

Other times, fun things happen by accident. Scientists were trying to make a rubber substitute when they invented another popular toy. It may be silly, but that's where the fun is!

What do you like to play with? Do you ever invent your own fun? Come and read about how people have been making fun for years.

Filling Up the Toy Chest

Fill up your toy chest with some of the best toys ever invented. What makes them such long-time favorites? They have few frills and need no batteries. All they need is you and your imagination.

Super toy

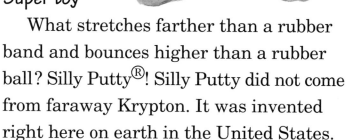

What stretches farther than a rubber band and bounces higher than a rubber ball? Silly Putty®! Silly Putty did not come from faraway Krypton. It was invented right here on earth in the United States.

During the 1940's, scientists working to create new types of rubber came up with something unexpected—a bouncing putty. No one could think of a way to use it. Then Paul Hodgson bought a supply, named it "Silly Putty," and sold it as a toy. Sales took off in leaps and bounds.

Silly Putty is a registered trademark of Binney & Smith Inc.

Spring into action

In 1943, American scientist Richard James was trying to develop a spring that would cushion the delicate instruments on ships as they rocked at sea. One day, a spring popped loose and began bouncing on the deck. James showed the bouncing spring to his wife, Betty, and she named it Slinky®. Two years later, the Jameses sold their first 400 Slinkies®. Now, the company they started, James Industries, turns hundreds of tons of steel into Slinkies® each year. They also come in colorful plastic models.

What's the word?

The word *marble* comes from *marmoros*, a Greek word meaning "shining stone." But the earliest marbles were made of baked clay, not stone. People have found clay marbles in prehistoric caves. The ancient Romans played games of marbles 2,000 years ago.

Who did it?

In the 1760's, an Englishman named John Spilsbury glued a map of Europe onto a sheet of wood, cut the map apart along the borders of the countries, and created the first picture puzzle. For years afterward, people used puzzles as teaching tools. In later years, the pictures on puzzles changed from maps to scenes from rhymes and stories, and a popular new toy was born.

Slinkies® have uses outside the toy box, too. During wartime, radio operators have tossed the metal wigglers over tree limbs to create makeshift antennas. Researchers have also used them on space shuttle missions to test the effects of weightlessness on springs.

Those bright, bold building bricks

The story of LEGO® building bricks began in 1949 in Denmark. A toymaker, Ole Kirk Christiansen, had just added plastic building bricks to his line of toys. At first, few people bought them. They preferred the traditional wooden toys for which Christiansen's company was known. But Christiansen and his son Godtfred kept improving the bricks and developed the "studs-and-tubes" lock by 1958. Then they produced sets of LEGO bricks for building towns, bridges, and vehicles. Soon, children all over Europe were enchanted with LEGO sets. LEGO building bricks spread far beyond Europe in later years. Some probably ended up right in your home. Today, people who visit the sights at Denmark's Legoland find out how far an inventive builder can go with LEGO building bricks.

LEGO is a registered trademark of INTERLEGO AG.

The Legoland amusement park in Denmark features model buildings and miniature scenes from around the world. Many of the attractions are built entirely of LEGO building bricks.

When and where

Board games date from at least 4,500 years ago. One ancient game was found in what is now Iraq, but no one today knows how to play it. Ancient board games we still enjoy include checkers, which began in Egypt about 4,000 years ago; chess, played about 1,300 years ago in India; and Parcheesi, another Indian game, which appeared in the late 500's.

Pie in the sky

Flying saucers fascinated a Californian named Walter Frederick Morrison. So he invented a "Flyin' Saucer" that skimmed through the air. In 1957, the Wham-O toy company began selling his saucer nationwide. How did a "Flyin' Saucer" become a Frisbee®? Many people say that the name comes from a game invented by college students in Connecticut—tossing empty pie tins from the Frisbie bakery through the air. However the toy got its name, by the mid-1960's, Frisbees® were selling in the millions.

Care to dance?

In 1958, Hula Hoops® hit the United States like a tropical storm. The Wham-O toy company made and sold 2 million hoops in only four months! Richard Knerr and A. K. Melin, owners of the Wham-O toy company, helped start the craze, but they did not invent the toy.

They had heard of a practice popular in Australia. People were twirling wood hoops around their waists as an exercise. Knerr and Melin started making the hoops out of lightweight plastic, hoping they might become popular in the United States, too.

Where did the name hula come from? Think of the Hawaiian hula dance. The motion that players make to spin a hoop around their waists so closely copies this dance that the word *hula* became part of the toy's name.

Haunting Melodies

What's the word?

Ciao is the way people who speak Italian say "hello" and "goodbye." Pronounce it "chow."

Music comes from the Greek word *mousa*, which means "muse." In Greek myth, the Muses were goddesses who ruled the arts and sciences. Terpsichore (turp SIHK uh ree) was the Muse of dancing, Calliope (kuh LY uh pee) was the Muse of epic poetry, and Polyhymnia (pahl ee HIHM nee uh) was the Muse of holy music. Can you find the roots of other English words in these names?

Ciao, my name is Cara, and I play with a band called Fancifulla. We haven't caught on in the United States yet, but we're getting very big in Italy.

Florence, Italy, is where my story takes place. Rosa, Giovanna, and I were setting up the equipment for our next show in a music hall. Then from out of nowhere came eerie groans.

"Did you hear that?" I asked Rosa.

"Spooky, Cara," Rosa said. "I think the place is haunted."

"It is I, Bartolomeo Cristofori." We all jumped.

"Cristowhoee?" Giovanna shouted.

Then I saw him, dressed in frills and ruffles and a wild white wig. I pointed and stammered, "Giovanna, look over there."

She piped right up. "Sir, you look pale! Want something to eat? You look like you could use some vitamins."

"I want to examine your *piano e forte*," he said. "You probably call it a 'piano.' The name has changed over the years since my death."

"He means the Kurzweil 2000R," I told the girls. Then I explained to the ghost,

"That's no piano; it's a synthesizer. It just sounds like a piano—and dozens of other instruments." Then I did a double-take. "Did you say you're dead?"

He fiddled with the keyboard, then he looked at me and smiled. "Yes, I died in 1731. But I come back now and then to observe the changes in my piano e forte. You see, I invented the first one right here in Florence around 1700."

"You invented the piano?" I was impressed. "Why do you call it a piano e forte?"

"Actually, the full name I gave my invention was *gravicembalo col piano e forte,*" Cristofori explained. "I'll say it again

—grah vee CHEM bah loh cohl pee AN noh ih FOR tay. It's Italian for 'harpsichord with soft and loud.' "

We must have looked puzzled because Cristofori went on. "Before my invention, the instrument closest to what you call a piano was a harpsichord (HAHRP suh kord). When the player struck a key, a special device inside the harpsichord plucked a tight wire, and the wire sounded a note. Plucking made all the notes from the harpsichord equally loud. I substituted hammer blows for plucking.

"This is how I did it: I linked each key to a system of levers. When the piano player hit a key, the levers took the movement of the key to a small hammer. The hammer struck a piano wire with the same force that the finger struck the key. So players could make soft notes or loud notes, depending on how hard they struck the keys."

"Awesome!" Rosa gushed. "You said something about changes. What kinds of changes?"

"One change was shape. My piano e forte was shaped like a harpsichord, which looks a lot like what you know as a grand piano. In 1811, Robert Wornum made a

Bright idea

The latest in portable music is the tiny personal compact disc player. Unlike larger models, this one fits in your pocket. And it will not skip a beat while you listen as you run or ride your bike. A computer chip in the player stores three seconds of upcoming music in its memory bank. So if you bump the player, the music keeps right on going.

smaller piano that looks like what you call an 'upright' today. Then in 1825, the piano e forte's wooden frame was replaced with an iron one. On an iron frame, a piano maker could pull the wires tighter and use

thicker wires than those used on wooden frames. The thicker wires made louder sounds."

"Who added pedals?" I asked.

"Different people did," Cristofori answered. "First there were levers that players could push to have loud or soft effects. Then in the 1780's, an English piano maker named James Broadwood put foot pedals on the piano. And in 1874, the Steinway brothers from New York improved a pedal that holds whatever notes the piano player chooses."

Then, just as suddenly as he appeared, Cristofori began to fade. His parting words sounded like, "Break a leg.* I'll be listening."

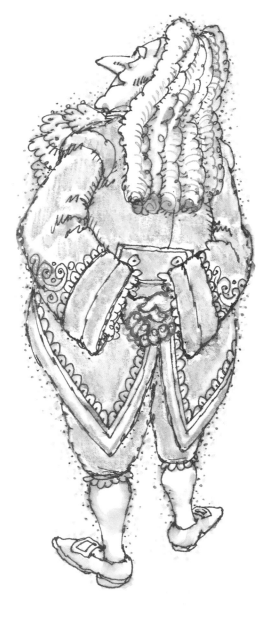

*Showbiz talk for "good luck"

54

YOU CAN DO IT!

Invent your own kind of music

Be sure you get your parents' permission before you start your band!

1. Gather some of the items listed at the right. Then, give these old standbys a new twist. Some suggestions follow.

2. Place stainless steel pot lids atop empty water glasses. Hit the sides of the lids with the knife to make them chime. Use several different sizes of lids to get a wide range of notes. Fill the gaps in the scale with pie tins or metal bowls over glasses.

Things you need:
- ✓ kitchen pots and lids
- ✓ water glasses
- ✓ butter knife
- ✓ pie tins
- ✓ empty plastic or glass bottles
- ✓ old, thin paint brushes

3. Make "wind instruments" by blowing across the tops of glass bottles or squeezing plastic bottles.

4. Imitate a jazz drummer and swish a brush or two on the bottom of a pot. Try the brush on other "drums," such as a cookie tin and an oatmeal box.

5. Use objects not mentioned here—and your imagination— to come up with other musical sounds.

6. Give a concert for friends and family with the instruments you invent.

You Great Big Beautiful Doll

Imagine a doll. Do you think of a cuddly baby doll? A soft rag doll? A glamorous fashion doll? Dolls have taken many forms during their long history. They were once very different from today's dolls.

The first doll-like figures appeared about 4,000 years ago in Egyptian tombs. For thousands of years before that, people had made figures representing their gods and goddesses. But the Egyptians were probably the first to make figures that stood for humans.

Egyptian "doll"

Children did not play with these dolls. Instead, the dolls were buried with high-ranking Egyptian officials to act as their servants in the afterlife. The dolls looked more and more realistic over the years. Archaeologists have found figures fishing from tiny boats, preparing bread, carrying food, and doing many other daily activities.

Greek and Roman children may have been the first to play with dolls. Soldiers made from wood, clay, or metal may have been playthings for Greek and Roman boys. The girls played with dolls that looked like women or babies.

Inventors of the earliest dolls are unknown. But we know the names of

Greek doll

What's the word?

An **archaeologist** (AHR kee ahl uh jist) is a person who studies life in ancient times. Few written records of those times have survived after so many years. So archaeologists examine household items, pottery, monuments, tools, and other remains to learn what life was like then.

Raggedy Ann doll

Mechanical
walking doll

many doll inventors in the 1800's and 1900's because they took out patents. For example, American Enoch Rice Morrison patented his design for a mechanical walking doll in 1862. Raggedy Ann is another American original. Cartoonist Johnny Gruelle patented his design for the famous rag doll with the yarn hair in 1915. He borrowed the name from two popular poems—"The Raggedy Man" and "Little Orphant Annie."

One doll who changes her hair style as often as her dress is also the best-selling doll ever. Do you know her name? If you guessed Barbie®, you're right.

Barbie was the idea of Ruth Handler. Handler was cofounder of Mattel Toys, and the mother of a young daughter who was more interested in fashions than in baby dolls. While traveling in Europe, Handler saw Lilli, a fashion doll from Germany. Then she realized what many American girls wanted—a doll that looked like a glamorous teen-ager with lots of clothes.

Who did it?

With their small rooms and tiny furniture, children and adults have loved dollhouses for hundreds of years. In the 1550's, the Duke of Albrecht of what is now Germany paid workers to build one of the first dollhouses. Tapestries covered the walls of the little mansion, and lovely silver or gold-plated objects were placed around the house. But no child ever played with it. The duke put it in his museum with models of villages and towns.

Colleen Moore's dollhouse at the Museum of Science and Industry in Chicago

When and where

GI Joe is the modern American version of the early Greek and Roman soldier doll. Joe began in 1964. At that time, he was nearly a foot (30 centimeters) high, with movable limbs and lifelike hair. Between 1978 and 1982, GI Joe dropped out of the toy scene. Then he made a comeback as a small plastic soldier, less than half the size of the first model.

Ruth Handler worked with Mattel employees to create an American version of Lilli. Only Handler's employees, who actually sculpted the doll's face and figured out how to make its joints bend, have their names on the patents for the doll. But Handler got to name the doll Barbie after her daughter.

Mattel introduced Barbie and her first line of outfits in 1959. Since then, the company has sold more than 500 million Barbies. She now ranks as the best-selling doll in history.

Barbie (second from right) and some of her friends

Trolls, on the other hand, could take the prize for being the ugliest dolls in history. These dolls are rooted in the folk tales of Denmark. According to Danish legend, the trolls spent their nights burying precious metals and gems. Humans seldom saw the trolls because they lived underground by day, guarding their treasure.

Troll doll

Thomas Dam heard these stories as a child. One year he carved a wooden troll for his daughter. In the 1960's, Dam brought vinyl versions of this troll doll to the United States. American kids loved them as much as his daughter had.

For a while, American-version trolls with long hair in many different colors were the latest craze. Then the little dolls disappeared from the toy scene, as if they had gone underground with their treasure. They reappeared in the 1990's, as popular as ever, and treasured by thousands of children.

Bright idea

Beulah Louise Henry invented two dolls for the price of one! "Miss Illusion" had blond and brown snap-on wigs, changeable eye color, and a reversible dress. Henry patented her two-for-one doll in the 1920's.

From the Velocipede to the 21 Speed*

The space vehicle from the planet Vorba hovered high over the earth. "Commander, our ship is over France," said the Vorban ensign.

"Zoom in on the Earthlings, Ensign Zork," said the commander. "We are here to gather data on their types of transportation."

"Yes, Ma'am. I now see several signs that read 'Tour de France,' and many Earthlings milling about. Some of them seem to be rolling along, with wheellike limbs!"

*Translated from the original Vorbish

"Wheellike limbs? Sounds crazy, Ensign. What does our databank say about this 'Tour de France'?"

"The Tour de France is a bicycle race held in France each year with racers from all over earth."

"What on Vorba is a bicycle, Ensign Zork?"

"According to the databank, the bicycle is a pedal-powered vehicle that moves on two wheels."

"Ah, that explains your wheellike limbs. What do you find about bicycles?"

"About 1817 (earth years), a German baron invented a bicyclelike scooter called the *draisienne* (dray SEHN). A pedaled version appeared about 1839. But it seems it didn't work too well. . . . Let's see—yes, here we are, Ma'am. I see two Frenchmen, Pierre and Ernest Michaux, in 1861. They are attaching more modern pedals to the front wheel of a newer-looking bicycle."

"Fast forward again, Ensign. Find out how successful this invention was."

"I see two Earthlings. Let's listen in," said the ensign.

"Here's to our Velocipede, Papa. We invented it only four years ago, and already we are manufacturing 400 a year."

"But it is not perfect, Ernest. The English call it a 'boneshaker.' The heavy frame and the wood-and-

metal wheels really jolt the riders over cobblestone streets."

"Keep scanning, Ensign Zork, and find out if those boneshaking wheels were fixed."

"Yes, Ma'am, I've found it. In 1869, British riders tested wheels with solid rubber tires. The rubber tires cushioned the ride. Englishman James Moore used a model with solid rubber tires to win one of the first bicycle races in 1869. Even riding a very heavy bicycle, he managed to go 83 miles (133 kilometers) in 10 hours, 25 minutes."

"Ensign, did bicycles ever lighten up?"

"I'm zeroing in now on a newspaper from 1873. It says that James Starley has made bicycle wheels with lightweight wire spokes. But the front wheels are very high. Let's see, in the years to come, the front wheels get higher and higher. Soon, the seats are so high, riders must lean their bicycles against buildings so they can climb up on them. The English laughingly call these bicycles 'penny-farthings' because the front wheel reminds them of their large penny and the back wheel of a *farthing,* their smallest coin.

"This penny-farthing looks nothing like the bicycles in modern France. Keep

Bright idea

By the 1890's, bicycle riders were using "dropped" handlebars that helped streamline their bodies. But the riders were so cramped that their knees almost knocked their noses while they pedaled. American cycling champ Major Taylor added an extension that pushed the handlebars forward. Today, Taylor's extension is standard equipment on racing bikes.

1934 Schwinn Streamline Aerocycle

looking, Ensign, there must be more changes."

"There are, Ma'am. An Englishman named H. J. Lawson made a bicycle with same-size wheels in 1873. He connected the pedals and the rear wheel with a chain drive. This invention was dubbed the 'safety bicycle' because it was safer than the penny-farthing to mount and ride.

"In 1888, Irishman John Dunlop developed air-filled tires. Next came coaster brakes, which operated by back pedaling, and gears, which let the rider change speeds."

"Back to the present, Ensign Zork. Let's find out how far bicycles have come. Have

Ensign Digo aim his viewfinder at the design department of a bicycle factory today."

"Yes, Ma'am, he's got it now. A blueprint there shows something called *derailleur* (dih RAY luhr) gears—gears that 'derail' the chain from one sprocket, or toothed wheel, to another. Derailleur gears give this model twenty-one speeds!

"Bicycle riding certainly has become faster, Ma'am, but I still don't understand why Earthlings prefer bicycles over rockets, for instance."

"Who knows! Maybe they just enjoy the ride."

When and where

The derailleur gear was developed in France around 1900. It was little used, however, until the 1930's, when bicycle racers began to use bikes equipped with derailleurs. Now, derailleurs are standard equipment on many bicycles.

T.V. TEASERS

Ted the Host: Hello everyone! It's time for TV Teasers, the game show where the viewers learn while the players earn. I am Ted, your host, and our players today are Keela and Mateo.

Players, you've proven that you know more than any other kids about almost everything. Now it's time for you to square off in the "Expert Round." Keela, you won the toss, so you choose the category. What will it be?

Keela: Let's try "Television History," Ted.

Ted: The first question is: What German inventor first sent the image of an object onto a screen in 1884?

Keela: Was it Paul Nipkow?

Ted: That's right! Keela, you now have $1,000. Mateo, the second question asks: How did the Italian inventor Guglielmo Marconi contribute to the invention of television in 1895?

Guglielmo Marconi

Mateo: Marconi was the first person to use radio waves to send messages. Later, similar waves were used to send TV signals.

Ted: Correct, Mateo. Now you also have $1,000. Do you want to risk it all on a "Double Dare"?

Mateo: I'll risk it, Ted.

When and where

The first video game package designed to be played on a television set at home was called "Odyssey." It came out in 1972.

Ted: Listen up: What did Karl Ferdinand Braun of Germany invent in 1897, and how did his invention work?

Mateo: Braun invented the cathode-ray tube. To do this, he painted the inside of a glass tube and put a part called a *cathode* in the tube. The cathode beamed electrical energy that made the paint glow.

Ted: He's phenomenal, folks! Now, Keela, this question is for you: What Russian-American inventor improved the cathode-ray tube and called it a *kinescope* (KIHN uh skohp)?

Keela: The inventor was Vladimir Zworykin.

Vladimir Zworykin

Ted: Yes! For $1,000 more: What was Zworykin's other invention for television?

Keela: Ummm. . . .

Ted: The clock is ticking, Keela.

Keela: Ummmm. . . .

(Buzz)

Ted: Keela, sorry, time is up. Mateo, can you tell us the name of Zworykin's other television invention?

Mateo: Zworykin and his staff invented an iconoscope (eye KAHN uh skohp) in 1923.

Ted: Good for you, Mateo. To reach a total of $5,000, answer the following question: What did the iconoscope do?

Mateo: The iconoscope was a camera tube. Part of the tube made an electric copy of the scene that the camera was recording. It changed bright and dark spots into strong and weak spots of electricity. An electric beam in the camera "read" the spots and turned them into strong and weak electric picture signals.

Ted: Right again! I can see why you two are finalists. What do you think, ladies and gentlemen? (Applause) Next, we play our free-for-all round. Each correct answer gets you $1,000. Here's the first question: How do the picture signals get from the camera to your television set?

Bright idea

The engineers at Philips Consumer Electronics in the Netherlands recently invented a way to make television watching more active—the Compact Disc-Interactive (CD-I). The CD-I player hooks onto your TV set and plays programs that invite you to take part. For example, one program lets you pretend you're actually touring museums. You have the sense of playing instruments, flying airplanes, and walking around statues, observing them from any angle you choose.

A color television test broadcast in 1950

(Ring, ring)

Ted: Keela.

Keela: The signals travel through the air from a broadcast antenna. Your television antenna receives them and sends them into the set, or your TV may receive signals through a cable.

Ted: Correct! Next question: What countries had regular TV broadcasting before the United States did?

(Ring, ring)

Ted: Keela again.

Keela: Germany and England.

Ted: Good job, Keela. The last free-for-all question pays triple or nothing. If you answer the question incorrectly, you lose all the money you have won. If you answer it correctly, you add $3,000 to your winnings, plus you get a special prize. Ready? Listen: When and where was the first color television broadcast?

(Ring, ring)

Ted: Take it away, Keela.

Keela: In the United States in 1953.

Ted: Congratulations, Keela! You have just won $7,000 and. . . (drum roll) a deluxe, super duper, big-screen, zillion-channel, cable-ready, remote-access, fully automatic Zoomatron color TV! Let's hear it for Keela, folks! (Wild applause)

EVERYDAY

INVENTIONS

Did you ever "rough it" in the wild, with only a tent and a few warm clothes? Did you warm yourself and cook your food over a wood fire, and drink from a stream when you were thirsty? If you've done these things, you know a little about everyday life without modern inventions.

Inventions are all around us. Things we use every day, from the time we brush our teeth in the morning until we turn down our blankets and crawl into bed at night, were invented by someone. Some everyday inventions make us more comfortable. Others make life easier for us. What are some of the inventions that we use every day and how were they invented? Read on, and find out!

Home Then, Home Now

Would your home have looked different if you were living seventy years ago? You bet. Compare inventions in a 1920's home with those in a modern home. You'll be surprised at the changes!

Toothbrushes

Yesterday's bathroom

- In the 1920's, enameled bathtubs were the newest thing. Many tubs had "claw feet" and exposed plumbing.

- Toilet paper was invented as early as 1857. An inventive manufacturer began putting it on a roll in 1871.

- Women were trying new, short hairstyles and permanent waves. Electric curling irons helped make these styles bouncy!

- Toothbrushes were made of boar's hair bristles. Toothpaste in a tube came out in the 1890's.

- Modern safety razors came out in 1903. They really caught on after soldiers started using them during World War 1 (1914-1918).

Safety razor kit

Electric curling iron

Today's bathroom

- Some shower-tubs of today have massage jets, stereo speakers, pillows, clocks, folding tray tables, and even speaker phones!

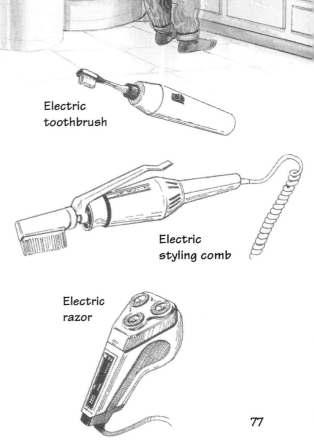

- In the United States, the first electric toothbrush became available in 1961, and companies first offered toothpaste in a pump dispenser in 1984.

- The first electric styling comb—a comb that blows warm air—was imported to the United States in 1965.

- The first successful electric razor was manufactured in 1931. Disposable razors were developed in France in 1974 and brought to the United States in 1976.

Electric toothbrush

Electric styling comb

Electric razor

Yesterday's kitchen

- An icebox, which contained a big block of ice, kept food cold. The first refrigerators were appearing by the late 1920's.

- Many 1920's stoves burned coal or wood. The small side section on the right is the "firebox" for the fuel.

- A percolater made coffee by boiling water. The water bubbled up through a hollow tube and dripped back down over the coffee grounds.

Percolator

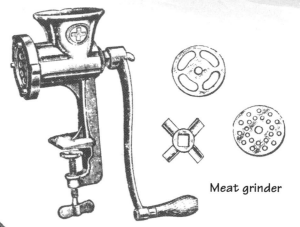

Meat grinder

- Most cooks in the 1920's had to put muscle into their work. They had to chop, stir, grind, and beat by hand.

- Most kitchens had floors of wood, tile, or a rubbery material called linoleum (lih NOH lee uhm).

78

Today's kitchen

- Refrigerators have changed since the first modern models came out in 1927. Today, many have water dispensers and ice makers.

- Microwave ovens were developed in the 1940's. But these handy machines didn't catch on until packaged foods for the microwave appeared in the 1970's.

- Homemakers still had to wax and buff kitchen floors until easy-to-clean no-wax floors came out in the 1970's.

- Dishwashers started to catch on in the 1950's. Today's dishwashers sterilize and dry dishes and dispose of food waste.

- The modern home food processor was developed in France in 1971. Automatic drip coffeemakers caught on in the 1970's.

Automatic drip coffemaker

Food processor

Yesterday's living room

- The first electrically recorded phonograph discs came out in 1925. A thin needle ran along grooves in the disc to make sound.

- Jigsaw puzzles, books, yo-yo's, kaleidoscopes, and *stereoscopes*, which showed 3-D images of interesting scenery, provided entertainment.

Stereoscope

Early telephone

- Most telephones had an attached mouthpiece to speak through and a trumpet-shaped ear piece. Sometimes you had to shout!

- The golden age of radio began about 1925. People gathered around the radio to listen to their favorite shows.

- Before air conditioning, great, open porches caught cool breezes in the summer.

Today's living room

- CD players came onto the market in 1983. These machines shine a laser beam onto discs to "read" a code for different sounds.

CD player with a disk

- Home air-conditioning systems became available during the 1930's. Many homes had air conditioning by the early 1980's.

- Telephone answering machines became popular for home use in the 1970's.

- In the 1950's, television took over radio's place in the home. VCR's became popular in the mid-1980's.

- The first home video game, Pong, bounced onto the scene in the 1970's. Nintendo® added to the fun in the mid-1980's.

**Nintendo®
video game**

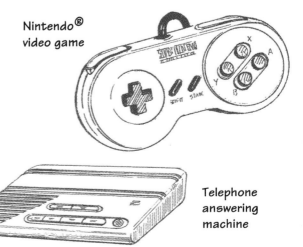

**Telephone
answering
machine**

Future Homes, Inc.

The Walker family waited in the office of Future Homes, Inc. They were startled by an amazing voice. It sounded tinny, but human, in a way.

"Welcome," said the voice. "My name is Randroid. I am not programmed to answer to 'Randy,' 'Randito,' or 'The Randster.' Follow me, and you'll see what home life might be like in the year 2020. Come along quickly. There is much to see."

Randroid rolled swiftly along on little rubber wheels. Nate and his younger

What's the word?

The Czechoslovakian playwright and novelist Karel Čapek invented the word *robot*. In Čapek's native language, the word *robota* means "drudgery," or boring work that most people would rather not do. What chore do you really dislike? Try drawing a plan for a robot that can help you with it.

brother Lewis struggled to keep up as Randroid led them across the lawn toward a brown brick house.

"This house doesn't look so different," Nate said as he stepped up to the door."

"Not so fast, young man," Randroid said. "Kindly place your feet on the welcome mat before you go in."

Lewis obeyed the robot's command. "It tickles," he said.

"Your shoes are being cleaned," said Randroid. "The mat uses special sound waves called *ultrasonic waves* to shake off the dirt."

"The house seems very comfortable," Mrs. Walker said as they all stepped inside. "And tidy!"

"I should say so," replied Randroid. "Light sensors trigger the windows to darken and lighten to maintain pleasant temperature and light levels. Other sensors note the dust content so automatic vacuums can suck it out."

"This is all done with sensors?" Mr. Walker asked with wonder.

"Sensors and robots like me," Randroid answered. "Most humans could not keep a house running as smoothly as a robot can. When I think of the dirt, clutter, and disarray humans cause, I shudder." His lights pulsed.

"Now for the living room." Randroid beeped, and the wall moved aside. The Walkers gasped. A television screen and stereo and computer equipment like the Walkers had never seen before lined the inner wall. There was also a fold-out workout station. "I see that you are impressed," said Randroid. "Here, you can challenge yourself with music or language lessons, a workout, or computer games matched to your level."

"There's a computer. At least I know how to work that," said Nate. "But wait! Where's the keyboard?"

"This computer is voice-controlled. You talk to it instead of typing commands. It

can help you with your homework, plan your workout, or set up the family budget."

"Is every room this advanced?" asked Mr. Walker.

"Yes, it is," replied Randroid. "Let us take a look at the kitchen. Instead of cooking, you can tell me what you want to eat. My software can plan healthy meals for the whole family. I can even suggest different ingredients to allow for allergies, special diets, and different tastes. I have ordered the refrigerator to be stocked with an assortment of food. Would you like a snack?"

"Yeah! Let's have a triple hot-fudge banana split!" Lewis piped up.

Randroid turned to the refrigerator and said, "Fruit snack, please. Include grapes, bananas, watermelon, and cherries."

Mrs. Walker nodded at Randroid with approval. In a moment, a small door opened. A cup of fruit salad sat on a tray. "At least you got bananas," said Nate.

"When you finish your snack, young man, simply put your cup in this cleaning cupboard," instructed Randroid. "Sensors will detect when the cupboard is full and start a cleaning cycle."

Mrs. Walker looked unconvinced. "So you can order food, plan meals, and clean up after," she said. "Can you do the same for laundry?"

CANS PAPER FOOD PLASTIC

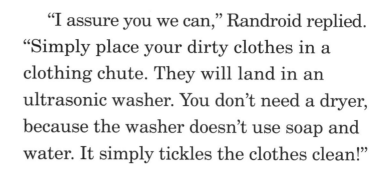

"I assure you we can," Randroid replied. "Simply place your dirty clothes in a clothing chute. They will land in an ultrasonic washer. You don't need a dryer, because the washer doesn't use soap and water. It simply tickles the clothes clean!"

"Like the welcome mat!" said Lewis.

"Exactly," said Randroid.

"There has got to be something you can't do!" exclaimed Nate. "Can you straighten up my room?"

"With ease," said Randroid.

"Can you start a shower at just the right temperature?" asked Mr. Walker.

Bright idea

Frances Gabe has been working on her design for a self-cleaning house since 1955. She began building one in 1974 in Newberg, Oregon. The house has waterproof furniture and a cleaning system in each room. To keep a room clean, you just push a button. Special cupboards and waterproof covers protect items that shouldn't get wet while the system cleans the rooms.

Frances Gabe in her kitchen

"I can program different temperatures for each family member." Randroid recited patiently. "I also can program the tub to clean itself after each use."

"What about wake-up calls?" Mr. Walker challenged.

"I can call you gently when it's time for you to get up. Then again," Randroid's panel lights flickered with mischief, "I can call you loudly, if you prefer. Of course, coffee, tea, juice, or milk will await you at your bed or kitchen table."

"Okay!" laughed Mrs. Walker. "There's nothing you can't do. I only have one more question: when can we move in?"

Clocks Whose Time Had Come

Some things happen over and over again and don't ever change. For example, the sun rises and sets every day. The seasons pass year after year. The moon grows bigger day by day until it's full, and then it gets smaller. Your heart beats in your chest with a steady rhythm, and waves crash on the shore. We call things that repeat in this way *cycles*. Believe it or not, people first learned to tell time—and to build clocks—by paying attention to the cycles they saw in nature.

The earliest, most ancient clocks simply reflected the sky's cycles for people to see. They were giant circles made of stones or other material that marked the passing of seasons and the movement of stars. Many scientists believe that Stonehenge, England's ancient grouping of huge stones, once served as such a "clock." At certain times of the year, the sun and moon would line up with certain stones. When this happened, the ancient people knew a new season had begun.

What's the word?

The word **clock** is actually related to words that mean "bell" in other languages, for example the Latin *clocca*, the Middle Dutch *clocke*, and the Middle German *glocke*. The earliest medieval clock towers had no hands to mark the hours. Instead, a bell rang out passing hours.

Stonehenge

No one ever thought about dividing days into equal parts until about 4,000 years ago. It was then that the idea of a 24-hour day was invented, probably by the ancient Babylonians. To measure the hours, they invented the sundial. A sundial is a circle with marks that show the hours between sunrise and sunset. A stem in the middle of the dial throws a shadow on the marks. As the sun travels across the sky, the shadow moves and shows the time.

But sundials were not always useful. For one thing, they only worked on sunny days. Even then, if you wanted to know what time it was, you had to run outside. And of course, sundials didn't work at nighttime at all!

Sundial

Then about 3,400 years ago, the Egyptians learned to create cycles that they could use to tell time. They figured out that water flows from a hole in a container at a steady rate. This idea led to the invention of the water clock. In early water clocks, water seeped out a small hole in the bottom of a stone container. Markings on the sides showed the hours. A person could tell time by the amount of water left in the container.

People were using sand clocks by the 1300's. They worked in much the same way as water clocks. The simplest sand

What's the word

The water clock was called a *clepsydra* (KLEHP suh druh), or "water thief," because it seemed to make water disappear!

93

clocks were two glass bulbs connected by a small "neck." Sand poured from the upper bulb to the lower. When all the sand had flowed from the upper bulb, a timekeeper knew that a certain amount of time had passed. Sand clocks that took an hour to empty were called *hourglasses*. Today's egg timers are small sand clocks.

Then, about 700 years ago, mechanical clocks first appeared in Europe. To mark the passing time, these clocks used rising and falling weights to turn a gear. The gear turned until it triggered the ringing

Sand clock

When and where

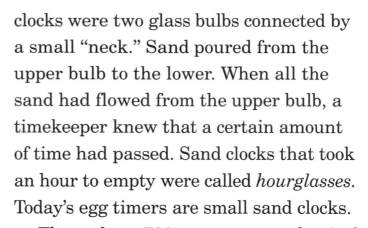

Clockmakers have come up with some surprising timekeepers through history. In the A.D. 800's, Alfred the Great, an English king, had a clock made from six 12-inch (30.5-centimeter) candles. The king's servants lit them one after another, and they burned at a rate of twenty minutes per inch. All six together lasted 24 hours.

In the late 1000's, the Chinese inventor Su Sung invented a clock run by a water wheel. It towered more than 30 feet (9 meters) and weighed tons. It showed the movement of the sun, moon, and stars. In 1126, invaders from the north took the giant clock apart and carried it away. It was never seen again.

In 1354, clockmakers finished a mechanical clock at the Cathedral of Strasbourg in France. This clock even performed! While bells played hymns, religious figures on the clock moved around. Every hour, a mechanical rooster in the clock of a bell. When holy men called *monks* heard the bell, they knew it was time to gather for prayer.

Mechanical clocks, like water clocks and sand clocks, measured hours as they passed. But the earliest mechanical clocks really didn't "tell the time." They had no dial or hands—they only gave a signal when an hour had passed. And they didn't even do that very well. The chiming was off by up to fifteen minutes a day.

Time-telling as we know it began in 1656, when a Dutch inventor, Christiaan

Bright idea

Louis Essen and J. V. L. Parry invented the atomic clock in 1955. They discovered that atoms vibrate more steadily than anything else in the world. Then they figured out a way to change these tiny vibrations into time information. An atomic clock is so accurate, it only loses or gains one second in 200,000 years!

crowed and flapped its wings. Only the rooster remains today.

Can you tell time with your nose? In the 1300's, some people in China could! They used a special "incense clock." It had a grooved path that looked like a maze. The path contained a variety of types of incense (a sticky substance that smells good when you burn it). The user lit the incense at one end, and each type burned for one hour. Each time the smell changed, the user knew an hour had passed.

The rooster from the Strasbourg clock

Huygens, developed a pendulum clock. He used the steady motion of a freely swinging pendulum to mark the time. The swinging of the pendulum is a more dependable cycle than dripping water or hanging weights. As a result, the pendulum clock was accurate to within about fifteen seconds a day!

Times change—even when it comes to telling time. Today's clocks are more accurate than anything Huygens could have imagined. Many run on electricity. Others use the steady vibrations of a tiny quartz crystal or even atoms to mark time.

YOU CAN DO IT!

Make your own time stick

Things you need:
✓ 3 pieces of 1" x 2" (2.5 x 5 cm) wood, one 3 in. (7.6 cm) long, one 17 in. (43 cm) long, and one 20 in. (51 cm) long
✓ wood glue
✓ black marker

17"

3"

20"

1. Lay the shortest piece of wood on top of the longest piece at one end. Glue it in place.

2. Form a T-shape by placing the medium-length stick on its side, on top of the short piece. Glue it in place.

3. Lay the stick on flat, level ground. If it is morning, the T-shape should face east. If it is afternoon, it should face west.

4. Note where the sun's shadow falls each hour and mark it with the black marker.

5. Amaze your friends with your homemade ancient clock!

Keep Your Shirt On!

You might think clothes were an important invention. And they were! But what good would clothes be if they kept falling off our bodies? Read about a few inventions that help us keep our clothes where they belong.

In 1893, Whitcomb Judson invented the sliding fastener, or zipper, to replace buttonhooks on shoes. The sliding fastener wasn't called a zipper until much later, though. In 1923, the Goodrich Company gave the name "Zipper" to boots that closed with a sliding fastener. People were much more charmed by the fastener than by the Zipper boots. Soon, everyone was calling the fastener itself a zipper. And the name stuck.

Makers of clothing place buttons for men's clothes on the right side and for women's on the left. No one is sure how this custom got started. Some say it let men unbutton their coats with the left hand and draw their swords with the right.

Walter Hunt never meant to invent the safety pin. But, so the story goes, he owed a man money. The man gave Hunt a piece of wire and offered him $400 for anything he could invent. Hunt twisted the wire into a safety pin. He patented it in 1849, and it's said to have made the man who bought it rich.

By the 1830's, a French cloth factory was making "woven elastic." Workers did this by weaving a thread of rubber through the cloth. Happily, woven elastic lets us have stretch waistbands. Lots of pants would fall down without them.

Where Would We Be Without. . . ?

All of these people are in big trouble! They need an invention to help them out. Can you name the invention that would rescue each person? The answers are listed at the bottom of the next page.

ACHOO!!

A.

B.

C.

D.

E.

BEANS

F.

INVENTIONS THAT CHANGED THE WORLD

Can you imagine what life would be like if people didn't know how to grow food and there were no farms? How would you eat? What if there were no computers or cars, or no ships that could sail across the sea?

It may surprise you to learn that there was a time when people had none of these things. Life was very different then, you can be sure.

This chapter tells about some inventions that have completely changed the way people live. In fact, the changes that these inventions brought about made the world a different place. As you read about the inventions in this chapter, look around at the inventions that are familiar to you. Then try to picture what the world would be like without them.

Starting a Civilization

Greetings, travelers! My name is Eureka. I travel through time with my horse, Discovery, and our flying chariot. What makes the chariot fly? You may think it's Discovery that pulls us up above the clouds! But this chariot is actually powered by your curiosity! The more you want to learn about amazing things, the faster and farther we can fly.

What's the word?

A **civilization** is a way of life that is highly developed in terms of its government, agriculture, trade, arts, and sciences.

Today, we will journey into the past to witness the birth of some of the world's most important inventions. Each of the inventions we'll see has shaped life on earth for thousands of years. They're probably part of your life today!

You might get dizzy spinning back in time, so hold on tight. Our first stop is about 500,000 years in the past! Do you see that glow far below us? It's a fire. The earliest people did not know how to start fires. Their nights were long and dark. They huddled close together under animal skins to keep warm. They didn't even have a way to cook food.

Then—no one knows exactly when—people invented tools to make fire. Perhaps someone noticed sparks that flew from two rocks striking together. This ancient inventor then may have tried hitting stones together so the sparks fell on dry grass. Later, people invented the bow-and-drill fire starter. They used the bow to whirl the drill against a piece of wood. The wood got hotter and hotter until embers formed. Then they used the embers to start a fire.

Once people learned to make fire starters, they could build a fire whenever they wanted. Fires provided light, warmth, and a way to cook food. Later,

Who did it?

Lighting a fire is a lot easier today than it was long ago, thanks to an English druggist named John Walker. In 1827, he invented one of the first matches. Walker's match was a wooden stick tipped with chemicals. It was hard to light, though. Many later matches were made with a chemical called phosphorus (FAHS fuhr uhs).

But these matches were more like fireworks. Striking them produced a bright shower of sparks and a cloud of bad-smelling smoke. Phosphorus was also poisonous. It wasn't until the early 1900's that inventors developed a match that adults could use easily and harmlessly.

people used fire to harden clay into pottery and to shape tools. Today, we use fire in many more ways. The fire of burning fuel powers the engines in our cars, boats, trains, and planes. Coal fires produce electricity at many power plants.

It's time to see another invention that was just as important. Close your eyes again and let your curiosity fly! Now we're moving forward in time. As the clouds part, look down and you'll see a family tending plants. These people lived about 11,000 years ago. They're some of the world's first farmers. Their garden is small and simple—almost wild. But eventually, farms will grow larger and become more organized.

Before people invented farming, they hunted, fished, and gathered wild plants for food. They had to move constantly, always searching for something to eat. They had little time to do anything else. After people learned to farm, they no longer had to travel to find food. They gathered in one place to tend their crops and built permanent places to live. These were the world's first villages. After a while, these villages grew into cities.

Farming also provided much more food for less work than before. With their free time, some people began to become experts in other types of work. Some became craftworkers, such as blacksmiths, potters, and weavers. Others became merchants, who made their living buying and selling goods that the craftworkers made. Still others devoted their energies to the arts. Music, sculpture, poetry, and drama began to develop.

Today, almost all of the food in the world comes from agriculture, and most people are free to do other things because farmers produce our food. Think about it—all the different jobs in the world were made possible at least partly because of agriculture.

Onward, Discovery! We're whirling forward again, to a time about 5,500 years ago in a place called Sumer (SOO muhr) in southwestern Asia. Look down there. Do you see the boy pulling the cart? The cart has wheels. You are witnessing one of the first uses of the wheel in the world. People made carts or wagons with two solid wooden wheels to help them move things. Later, they invented lighter spoked wheels for wagons and speedy chariots.

Today, we depend on wheels in endless ways. Of course, cars and trains roll along on wheels. But what about wheelbarrows, skateboards, tractors, and airplanes? And did you know that many machines—everything from engines to

lawn sprinklers to elevators—rely on
wheels to make them work? Gears and
pulleys are wheels, too. Even the knobs
on radios are wheels!

Now as we fly home, think about this:
Each of the inventions we have seen was
invented many times, by different people
in different places. These inventors lived
long before written records were kept, so
we will never know who they were. But
these nameless inventors have shaped
our lives.

No More Horsing Around

Howdy! My name is Hester. My great-great grandparents had jobs pulling carriages. They had lots to do. Everybody appreciated them. But things are harder for me. Workhorses have been replaced by the "horseless carriage"—the automobile!

Of course, folks didn't take to the automobile right away. No sir! People had been using horses for thousands of years. They weren't about to give up a good thing for that weird contraption.

Back in 1769, Nicolas-Joseph Cugnot, a Frenchman, built the first road vehicle that didn't need an animal to move it. His vehicle was powered by steam, and what a sight it was! No one had ever seen a carriage move under its own power before!

For many years after that, people experimented with steam carriages for transportation. Many people didn't like the new vehicles, though. The early steam engines were smoky, sputtery noisemakers that frightened horses! Besides, they couldn't pull plows and do other honest, important work that horses did.

In the 1880's, two German inventors both invented gasoline engines that were much better than steam-powered ones. Karl Benz and Gottlieb Daimler (DYM luhr) mounted their engines in three- or

What's the word?

Before automobiles, the word *car* could mean any vehicle on wheels. Car comes from a Latin word that means "two-wheeled wagon," "chariot," or "cart."

Who did it?

In the 1920's, an Italian named Enzo Ferrari worked for the Alfa Romeo automobile company. One of Ferrari's jobs was to race the company's sports cars.

In 1929, Ferrari left the company to start his own racing team of Alfa Romeos. Then in the mid-1940's, he decided it was time to make his own sports car. In 1946, his company unveiled the first of its sleek, speedy, stylish new brand of sports cars. His car was called—what else?—the Ferrari.

four-wheeled vehicles that looked like the carriages horses pulled. You can see why folks called them "horseless carriages"!

Back in those days, horses had lots of work to do because most people still drove around in horse-drawn carriages. The truth is, horses were faster and more reliable than the first cars. For a while, horses shared the streets with cars, but things were not always friendly. People who rode past a car stuck in the mud might yell "Get a horse!" to the driver. Farmers got sick and tired of the new cars spooking their horses. Some communities passed laws to prevent this. One required a person to walk ahead of a car with a red flag as a warning that a car was coming.

Unfortunately, the farmers were fighting a losing battle. An American named Henry Ford introduced a car called the Model T in 1908. In 1913, he finished setting up a moving assembly line in his factory. That way, he could make cars faster at a lower cost. Suddenly, even people who weren't wealthy could afford a car. Henry Ford built Model T's until 1927 and sold more than 15 million of them. People relied less and less on horses. Our days as important members of the work force were coming to an end.

Today, there are about 450 million cars in the world! People sure have changed their minds about "the horseless carriage"!

The assembly line at the Model T manufacturing plant

Whole cities are built differently because of the automobile. They are larger, and have more roads. Chances are, you live in a *suburb,* which is a community on the outskirts of a large city. Suburbs didn't even exist before cars were invented. That's because before there were cars, people had to live near the places where they worked. Today, people can live far away from their workplaces because the automobile makes getting back and forth possible.

Sure, cars are useful. But I'm out of work. It's not fair—no car has a soft nose and big brown eyes like mine. And I'm cheap—I run on oats and water! If you hear of any job openings, let me know.

When and where

Think about how many changes the invention of the automobile led to! Just ride down any street or highway in your town. Can you imagine how things would look if there were no cars?

In the past, some city roads had cobblestones or other rough pavement. Most country roads were dirt roads. Automobiles, with their higher speeds and rubber tires, ran better on smoother roads. As more people bought cars, communities began to pave their roads and build new roads. Roads have changed the landscape in almost every country.

All along the roadways, you see things that were invented because of the automobile. The first gas stations were in business by 1910. The motor hotel—or motel—was invented in the 1920's to serve people who needed to stop and rest during long car trips.

The first drive-in restaurant served motorists in Dallas in 1921. In New Jersey in 1933, Richard Hollingshead, Jr., opened the first drive-in movie theater, which let people enjoy movies from the comfort of their cars.

SOUND HORN WHEN
READY TO ORDER

HAMBURGER 1.35
CHEESEBURGER 1.50

DRINKS .50 .75 1.00
HOT DOG 1.00

Cutting Computers Down to Size

Liz has lots of fun with her family's computer. She plays games and types homework assignments on it. Liz's older brother writes music on it. Her mom calls the computer her "best friend" because it helps her plan the family budget. Liz calls it "George." And no one else in the family knows it, but George is a magic computer. Whenever Liz has a question, she asks George—and George answers!

One day, Liz wanted to find out about the invention of the computer. "Good morning, George," Liz typed. "I have a question."

"Good morning, Liz! Ask away!" The words glowed on Liz's computer screen.

"Who invented the computer?"

In an instant, George's answer was displayed on the screen.

"No single person invented the computer. Many people helped develop it over the course of many years." George's screen flickered. "Press the 'Enter' key for more information."

Liz pressed "Enter," and words filled the screen.

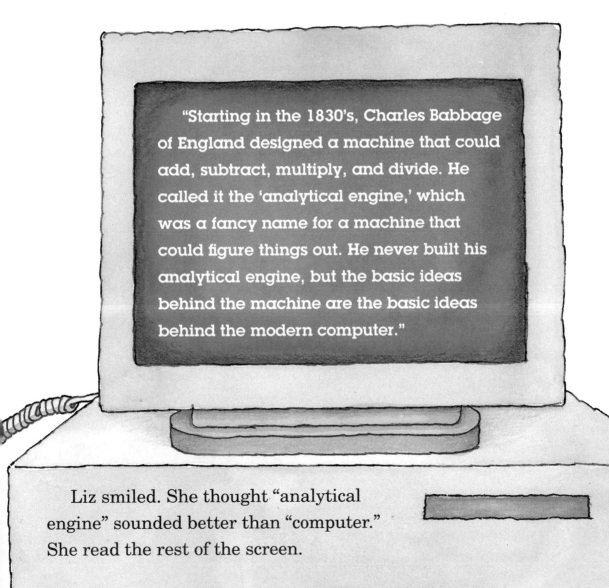

"Starting in the 1830's, Charles Babbage of England designed a machine that could add, subtract, multiply, and divide. He called it the 'analytical engine,' which was a fancy name for a machine that could figure things out. He never built his analytical engine, but the basic ideas behind the machine are the basic ideas behind the modern computer."

Liz smiled. She thought "analytical engine" sounded better than "computer." She read the rest of the screen.

Punch-card computer

"In the 1880's, Herman Hollerith of the United States invented a machine that used paper cards with holes punched in them to process large amounts of information. This machine was the first successful computer.

ENIAC

What's the word?

ENIAC stands for Electronic Numerical Integrator And Computer. (An integrator is a machine that performs calculations using certain kinds of numbers.) Enormous ENIAC weighed more than 30 tons (27 metric tons). That's about the same as six full-grown male elephants!

"American engineers J. Presper Eckert, Jr., and John W. Mauchly finished building ENIAC, the 'grandmother' of the modern electronic computer, in 1946. ENIAC could add thousands of numbers in seconds, but it was so big it filled an entire room."

Liz was puzzled. "How did people fit them in their homes?" she typed.

"They didn't," George replied. "In those days, computers were so large and expensive that only the government, big companies, and some universities had them."

"How did computers get to be your size, then?" Liz asked.

"The 'brains' of early computers were made of lots and lots of wires and fairly large working parts called *vacuum tubes*. But over the years, engineers invented ways for computers to store and process information in smaller and smaller spaces. If you look inside me, you would see that my 'brain' is a small chip about

What's the word?

In computer talk, when a system stops working, we say it has **crashed.** One of the things that causes a crash is a **bug,** or a mistake in a program. In 1945, one of the earliest computers broke down. Workers found that a dead moth inside was blocking the electrical signal. Ever since then, people have called problems with computer programs "bugs."

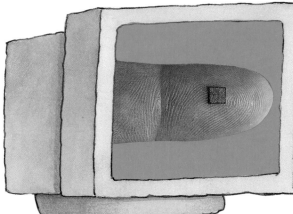

the size of the tip of your finger. Inventors took advantage of these improvements to develop faster, smaller, cheaper computers. The first personal computers came out in the 1970's. Now, computers are everywhere, and they are used in countless ways."

Liz asked him, "What ways?"

George responded right away. "Computers are used in almost every part of modern life. People use computers to learn things and to help solve problems.

Bright idea

Martine Kempf of France wanted to help people with disabilities. She thought a computer that responded to voice commands would be easier for disabled people to use. So, in 1982, she invented the Katalavox. She made up this name from the Greek word *katal,* which means "to understand," and the Latin *vox,* for "voice."

The Katalavox is a special computer that understands human voice commands. People who can't use their arms may be able to use this device to control wheelchairs or other machines.

A voice-controlled computer workstation

Computers perform calculations rapidly and can store large amounts of information. Millions of computers are at work throughout the world.

"Computers control traffic lights, teach in schools, guide ships, create artwork, help doctors diagnose illness, do scientific research. . . ."

The screen went blank for a second, then these words appeared:

"How much time do you have?"

Liz laughed. Someone had programmed George to be funny! But she had gotten the point: Computers have changed the world!

Today, people use computers to predict the weather (top), to help treat illness (center), and to teach in schools (bottom).

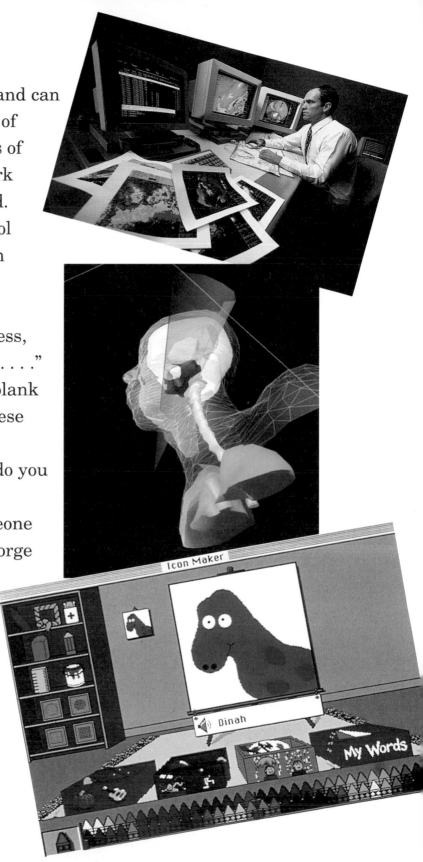

123

Sailing into History

Matthias settled down creakily in his rocking chair and spread a blanket over his knees. Beatrice and Tommy loved their old neighbor's stories about his days as a sailor on the high seas. "I've seen the noisy markets of the East, the deep-green coastlines of South America, the towering glaciers of the North," he would tell them. "I've seen waves as high as a two-story building and sunsets red as fire. I know firsthand what a grand and big place the world is."

For centuries, the sailing ship ruled the seas. Then, in 1769 in Scotland, James Watt patented an improved steam engine. Inventors soon tried to use steam to power ships. The first truly successful steamboat was American Robert Fulton's *Clermont*. In 1807, the *Clermont* made a successful run on the Hudson River in New York. Within 100 years, steamboats had all but replaced sailing ships on long ocean trips.

Today, steamships transport people and goods all around the world, just as the old sailing ships did hundreds of years ago. But steamships can cross the oceans in a fraction of the time that sailing ships needed.

"You worked on a steamship, right, Matthias?" asked Tommy.

"I did indeed," Matthias replied.

"Well, our father says sailing ships were one of the most important inventions ever. How can this be true?" asked Beatrice. "You told us people hardly use them anymore for long ocean voyages."

"Your pappy is right!" said Matthias. "The sailing ship was invented long ago. But the changes it led to are still important today. It made the world a smaller place." Tommy and Beatrice waited for him to continue, trying to picture how the world could shrink.

Matthias scratched his old, gray head. "Before the days of sailing ships, most

Wooden model of an
Egyptian sailing ship

What's the word?

The **hull** is the body of a boat, the part that floats in the water.

The **rudder** is a flat, movable piece of wood or metal that extends under the water on the rear of a ship. In old-fashioned ships, sailors moved a bar called a *tiller* attached to the rudder to steer.

people didn't know much about the world. They never traveled more than a few miles from their homes."

Matthias went on to tell Beatrice and Tommy about the history of sailing. They learned that the first seafarers were Pacific islanders. "More than 5,000 years ago, they braved the ocean in large canoes," said Matthias. "At about the same time, the Egyptians probably invented the first sailboats. My, they were graceful craft, with a single square sail and a hull of reeds or wooden planks."

Matthias described how sailing ships slowly improved. Shipbuilders designed stronger hulls and better sails. But most ships could not make great ocean voyages.

Then about 800 years ago, people in northern Europe began improving sturdy ships called *cogs*. "They were simple vessels but seaworthy!" said Matthias. Cogs stretched up to 100 feet (30 meters) long. They were wide and deep to stand up to mighty ocean waves.

Cog

Cogs were better in another way, too. Sailors used oars to steer earlier ships. But these new, improved cogs had a single rudder, like ships today. "The rudder was a great invention!" declared Matthias. "Rudders were stronger than oars, and better for steering a boat through rough seas."

When and where

Can you imagine trying to find your way across the sea? In the middle of the ocean, there's nothing to tell you which direction to sail or where you've come from. You look around you, and all you see is endless, unchanging water.

Instead of looking around to navigate (find their way) across the ocean, sailors of long ago looked up! They used the sun and stars to help them. One ancient invention that helped sailors navigate was the *astrolabe* (AS truh layb). Sailors used the astrolabe to measure the positions of planets and stars. With this information, they were able to figure out the position of their ship.

Early sailors also used compasses to tell direction. The first compasses were just small magnets on a piece of cork or straw floating in a bowl of water. Eventually, sailors came up with better ways of navigating, using special equipment. Today, ships use signals from satellites to figure out their position at sea.

Lateen sail

What's the word?

The triangular sail called the **lateen** got its name from the French word for "Latin sail." People in northern Europe heard about the sail from people in southern Europe near the Mediterranean Sea. This area had once been the center of the Roman Empire, and Latin was its language.

Cogs had square sails. But ships used by Arabs and people living along the Mediterranean Sea had triangular sails. They called these sails *lateens* (luh TEENZ). Using a lateen sail let ships sail more easily into the wind. With square sails, sailing into the wind meant slow zigzagging across the path of the wind. Triangular sails allowed the ships to sail in a straighter line, with less zigzagging. "This is mighty important!" Matthias told them. "Take it from an old sea dog: The wind doesn't always blow in the direction you want to sail!"

By about 1450, European shipbuilders developed a new kind of ship called the *caravel*. The caravel took the best features of the cog and added lateen sails. The result was a ship that could sail for months at sea. "In fact, the great ships of Columbus and other European explorers were caravels," said Matthias.

Caravel

Matthias leaned back in his chair and smoothed his blanket with his strong, old hands. "Those great sailing ships carried goods from far away. They brought home plants and animals, spices and treasures people had never seen before. They carried people too—settlers and explorers alike—to new lands. The world got smaller as travel became easier, and countries far away from one another carried on trade. And they didn't only trade goods. They traded ideas and people too."

Tommy and Beatrice sat quietly. They finally understood. "The world didn't really shrink," Beatrice said. "People just got to know it better, right, Matthias?" Matthias answered with a snore.

SAFETY

As strange as it may sound, living can be hazardous to your health. Think about it. There are storms, car accidents, fires, earthquakes, germs that can make you sick, and other dangers.

Lucky for us, many men and women have worked hard through the years to make life safer for everyone. It's easy to forget that some familiar inventions, such as seat belts, helmets, and fire sprinkler systems, are there to protect your health and life. Just try to imagine living without them. The people who invented these and other lifesavers are some of the world's great heroes.

Drive Alive

What do you think it was like to ride in a car a hundred years ago? It must have been exciting, but pretty scary, too. In those days, most roads were unpaved, and cars had no seat belts. Just staying in the seat wasn't easy as you bumped along dirt roads. Brakes were not as good as they are today. And because cars had no windshield wipers, snowy and rainy days were especially difficult. Without safety glass and airbags, even minor accidents could be pretty hard on the driver and passengers, too.

Luckily, cars have changed a lot since then. As more and more people took to the road, it became clear that something had to be done to make driving safer.

Only when cars could move faster did people come up with the idea of a "windscreen" to keep dirt, dust, and bugs out of the driver's eyes. The first windshields did this, but they led to a more serious problem: In accidents, shattered glass caused more injuries.

Safety glass came to the rescue. When this special three-layer glass breaks, the pieces stick to the middle layer and don't fly off.

Who did it?

Early traffic lights had two colors—green and red. Red meant "stop," of course, and green meant "move." But what about the yellow light? American inventor Garrett Morgan patented a three-color traffic signal in 1923. It looked very different from today's traffic lights, but gave a warning that the signal was about to change. This way drivers would know to "proceed with caution."

Garrett Morgan with his son and grandson

Now that cars had windshields, they needed windshield wipers. Mary Anderson of Alabama patented an idea for wipers in 1903. After seeing a shivering New York streetcar driver step off his car again and again to wipe snow from the front window, Anderson drew a plan for her "window cleaning device." Her handy invention could be operated with a lever from inside.

Edward J. Claghorn patented a lap safety belt in 1885. Claghorn probably wanted the belt to help keep passengers from falling out of horse-drawn buggies. To improve the lap belt for cars, Nils Bohlin of Sweden developed the shoulder belt about 1958.

Airbags, which are becoming more common in all cars, were developed in the 1960's. Here's how they work: If a head-on crash occurs at about twelve miles (19.2 kilometers) per hour or faster, the airbag instantly fills up with a gas called *nitrogen*. Airbags cushion the passengers in the front seat, keeping them from hitting the dashboard and windshield.

Now there are safer tires, too. When roads are wet and slick, it can be hard to stop or steer a car. These new rubber wonders have a wide, deep groove in the center. The water that's in front of the moving tires is forced into the groove and out to the sides. This creates a dry path

When and where

One day in 1903, a French scientist, Edouard Benedictus, accidentally dropped a glass flask. Instead of shattering, though, all the pieces of glass stuck together. Earlier, the flask had held a chemical called *cellulose nitrate* (SEHL yoo lohs NY trayt). Benedictus had an idea. He put together a "sandwich" of two sheets of glass and a middle layer of *celluloid*, a plastic made from cellulose nitrate. It was the first safety glass.

for the tires, making the car easier to control.

What does the future hold for car safety? By the time you're old enough to drive, carmakers hope that the following features will be available on all new cars:

- "Heads up" instrument displays. To help drivers keep their eyes on the road, the displays would be projected at the bottom of the windshield.
- Electronic collision warning systems that can alert a driver if the car is about to crash into another car.
- "Smart cars" that help drivers avoid traffic jams. Instruments in the car could figure out its location using satellite signals. A video screen in the car would then show the driver the fastest route while, a *synthesized* (artificial) voice gives directions.

55 MPH
TANK FULL

Bright idea

You board a train to take you to a city 245 miles (392 kilometers) away. As you travel, houses, farms, and buildings whiz past your window. Ninety minutes later, you arrive at your destination. This is three to four times faster than if you had gone by car. Considering travel to and from the airport, it's even faster than taking an airplane. You must be living in the year 2050, right? Not necessarily.

The future of high-speed trains is now. In fact, Japan has had such a train for almost 30 years. In 1965, "bullet" trains, named for their speed and appearance, began making high-speed runs between Tokyo and Osaka.

The success of the Japanese trains started a trend in high-speed trains around the world.

The TGV (train a grande vitesse— French for "the fast train") opened in 1981 between Paris and Lyons, in France. A high-speed train that can use existing tracks will soon run in the United States.

But are high-speed trains safe? You bet—and for a number of reasons. First of all, they run on electricity instead of fuel. Electric power is less harmful to the environment. And the more people travel on trains, the less they need to drive on crowded highways. Lighter traffic could mean fewer car accidents and less air pollution from car exhaust.

So far, high-speed trains have a very good safety record. Not a single injury or death has been reported on France's system.

What a way to ride!

What's the word?

Bacteria are very tiny *organisms*, or living things. They have only one *cell*, which is the smallest building block of all living things. Bacteria live all around us. Many kinds are harmless—or even helpful. But other kinds spoil food and make people sick. When we talk about one of these organisms, we call it a *bacterium*.

Beating Up on Bacteria

Shoving and scrambling to get the best seat, a group of young bacteria of all kinds—spunky spirals, rounds, and rods—crowded around their great-great-grandma. Grandma Bacterium had promised to tell them about their family history—the story of the glory days when bacteria could spread freely in food. That was before humans learned how to wipe them out—before life changed forever.

A hush settled on the gathering as Grandma B. began to speak. She told the youngsters that they weren't like other bacteria. "No, my pretties. We're special. We're harmful to humans, not like those goody-goody bacteria. We ruin food and cause disease, and we love it!" Grandma B.'s voice, a cross between a hiss and a gurgle, grew louder. "You must learn your history and be proud!" she declared. "The future of our kind is in your hands."

Grandma's story began when bacteria's powers were first discovered. "I'll never forget when I heard the news," Grandma B. recalled. "At long last, we got credit for causing all sorts of nasty trouble. Louis Pasteur, a French scientist, broke the story. He called us 'little nothings . . . that carry disease and death.' We couldn't have been more flattered!

"Well, we were feeling pretty good, spoiling food and spreading disease like never before. But then Pasteur tricked us! He figured out a way to control us." The youngsters saw that Grandma's anger toward Pasteur still burned.

Bruno, one of the tougher little bacteria, spoke up. "Tell us how he tricked you, Grandma B."

"Well Bruno, it wasn't pretty," said Grandma. "In the 1860's, Pasteur found he could do away with us by heating our homes—milk, cheese, and other foods— for a certain amount of time. And, oh, the cruel humans thought this was just so wonderful. They even named the evil process after him: pa . . . pa . . . pa. . . pasteurization (PAS chuhr uh ZAY shuhn)."

BOING

Grandma could barely make herself speak the word.

After a long pause, she calmed down and continued. "But that was just the beginning of our downfall. Once Pasteur announced that bacteria caused disease, others tried to find ways to fight us, too. A New York doctor named Hervey Thatcher patented a milk bottle in 1885. With this bottle, people could keep milk fresh longer. What a tease that bottle was! There was the cozy, tasty milk sealed up

Who did it?

In 1895, the French Emperor Napoleon offered a prize of money to anyone who could invent a new way to store food for French troops. Nicolas Appert, a chef, packed foods into glass containers. Next, he experimented with boiling and reboiling the airtight containers. The process worked! Appert had invented canning, which preserves food, and he won the money.

When and where

Keeping food fresh and tasting good has always been a challenge. Drying is probably the oldest method of preserving food. In warm climates, people dried fish, meat, fruits, and other foods in the heat of the sun. After fire was discovered, people began to use fire to dry some foods. This practice became known as smoking. People found that smoking not only dried the food but changed the taste. And they liked it!

in front of our noses, and we couldn't get inside. It was one of our family's darkest hours! We declined by the zillions.

"If that wasn't bad enough, in the early 1920's, another American human, Clarence Birdseye, developed a way to freeze us out."

The young bacteria shuddered. Pettice, a tiny cousin, piped up. "How did he know we couldn't survive the cold?"

"The way the story goes," Grandma replied, "Birdseye was on a fur-trading trip to Labrador, in Canada. He noticed that fish kept outside in temperatures below zero froze quickly. After the fish thawed, they still tasted good. Then Mr.

Know-It-All Birdseye experimented with ways to freeze fish as quickly as possible to keep its flavor and not give us bacteria a chance to multiply."

Grandma B. began to cry. "The worst part is that humans will keep looking for better ways to stop us. What are we to do?" Pretending to be brave, the little bacteria oozed closer to dry Grandma B.'s tiny tears. But inside, they were scared. Maybe they would never get a chance to spoil food and spread disease. What would life be like then?

The Pathway to Penicillin

Have you ever heard of a powerful drug called penicillin (PEHN uh SIHL ihn)? If you've ever had an ear infection, strep throat, pneumonia (noo MOHN yuh), or certain other kinds of infections caused by bacteria, penicillin has probably come to the rescue!

1928

Mold drifts through an open window into the laboratory of Sir Alexander Fleming, a British doctor, and lands on a dish of bacteria that he has been growing. Mold is a fungus, like mushrooms and mildew, that grows on plants or other matter. Fleming notices that where the mold is, the bacteria have died. He calls the mold *penicillin*. Because of its bacteria-killing power, Fleming believes it might be useful as a medicine. He grows penicillin mold in liquid, but he is not able to make it into medicine.

Sir Alexander Fleming and his life-saving mold

This "miracle drug" is one of the most important discoveries in medicine. It was the first germ killer that was safe for the patient. It took a long time to develop penicillin into a safe, useful medicine, and many people lent a hand. Let's take a look down the pathway to penicillin.

Ernst Chain

1938

Two British scientists, Howard Florey and Ernst Chain, come across Fleming's forgotten findings and develop the first penicillin drug.

Howard Florey (center) and a physician check on a soldier being treated with penicillin.

1939

World War II begins. Research on penicillin becomes more important because of the need for medicine for sick and wounded soldiers.

1941 Florey, Chain, and a British physician achieve the first major success in treating a patient with penicillin. A policeman nearly recovered from blood poisoning after receiving penicillin. Unfortunately, he died when the supply ran out.

1942

A Connecticut mother, Anne Miller, becomes the first person to be cured using penicillin. Anne was near death with a fever of 106 degrees Fahrenheit (41° Celsius). Her doctors got a small supply of penicillin from a laboratory where penicillin research was going on. Within 24 hours of receiving the penicillin, Anne's infection was gone.

Anne Miller and Fleming

The Nobel Prize medal for medicine

1945

The King of Sweden presents Fleming, Chain, and Florey with the Nobel Prize for medicine for their work in the development of penicillin.

Fleming (left), Chain (center), and Florey (right)

1949

British medical researcher Dorothy Crowfoot Hodgkin discovers the chemical makeup of penicillin. This makes it possible for partly *artificial* (human-made) penicillin to be made.

The Nobel Prize medal for chemistry

Dorothy Crowfoot Hodgkin with a diagram of a penicillin molecule

1964

Hodgkin wins the Nobel Prize for chemistry for her life's work, including her contribution to the development of penicillin.

Penicillin mold

Child receiving penicillin shot

Today

Doctors use penicillin to treat a wide range of dangerous illnesses caused by bacteria. Because it stops infections, penicillin also helps make surgery and other treatments safer.

Scanning the Skies

Hurricanes, tornadoes, and other violent storms can do terrible damage. Imagine homes being destroyed, trees uprooted, and entire communities flattened. We can't prevent these natural disasters from happening. But with the help of radar and artificial satellites, scientists can predict when and where storms are going to strike. With enough warning, people can take safety precautions.

Radar works like an echo. If you were to call out your name in a place surrounded by mountains, sound waves would travel out to the mountains. Then the sound waves would bounce off the mountains and come back to you as an echo. In the same way, radar sends signals in the form of invisible waves of energy. Radar waves hit objects in their path. Reflections—or echoes—of the waves bounce back to the radar. The radar then "sees" the object, which shows up as an image on a screen.

Scientists can use radar to track storms. Radar waves hit raindrops and ice in the air. From the echoes that come back, scientists can tell how strong a storm is, in what direction it's moving, and how fast it's traveling.

Like so many inventions, radar developed over time. You might say it started in the 1860's. At that time, British scientist James Clerk Maxwell stated the theory that invisible waves of energy of great power and speed existed.

In an airport control tower, radar equipment helps locate storms and direct airplane traffic.

In the 1880's, Heinrich R. Hertz, a German scientist, proved Maxwell's theory. Hertz discovered that Maxwell's invisible waves could be bounced off objects. This discovery led many scientists to believe that there had to be a way to use the waves to detect distant objects.

In 1935, Sir Robert Watson-Watt, a Scottish scientist, developed the first complete system for detecting distant ships and aircraft—often considered the first radar. And from then on, the uses for radar grew and grew. Scientists first used radar for weather observation during the 1940's.

Most airports have radar equipment to spot troublesome storms. Storm-tracking can help air traffic controllers warn pilots away from dangerous areas. If the storms can't be avoided, at least pilots can prepare themselves and their passengers.

Engineers developed another weather detector, the artificial satellite, in the 1960's. A satellite is an object that travels in a regular path around another object in space.

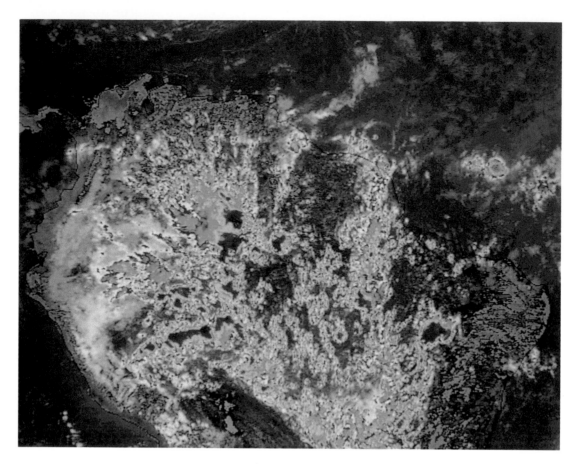

This satellite image shows thunderstorms as white "blobs" over a region of South America. The red and yellow spots are high clouds.

This means the moon is a natural satellite of the earth. Scientists build artificial satellites and send them into space.

Out in space, these satellites can tell us many things. Weather satellites have cameras that take pictures of the clouds. They can also measure wind speeds. This information helps scientists predict what kind of weather will happen all over the world. Suppose you looked outside now. Whether the weather is sunny, cloudy, rainy, snowy, windy, or calm, chances are a satellite "saw it coming."

When and where

Radar and artificial satellites help predict storms. But what inventions do we use to predict earthquakes? None, yet. But there is a machine that lets scientists detect earthquakes and measure their strength. It's called a *seismograph* (SYZ muh graf).

Earthquakes result from movement under the earth. Parts of the earth's rocky shell sometimes break and shift, making "waves" in the ground. These waves are earthquakes.

In 1855, Italian scientist Luigi Palmieri built the first device to record earthquakes. But it wasn't very helpful. Almost anything could cause Palmieri's invention to shake—an earthquake or even a cart rumbling along a road nearby.

Twenty-five years later, John Milne, an English scientist, started working on an earthquake detector. While teaching in Japan, a land of many earthquakes, he and his co-workers developed the first seismograph. Scientists use modern versions of Milne's seismograph today.

However, seismographs only determine the location of earthquakes and measure their strength. Scientists are still trying to create an invention that can predict earthquakes. Such an invention would make the earth safer for the millions of people who could be affected by a serious earthquake.

A scientist reads a printout from a seismograph.

Whistle While You Work

Hanging from the side of a building or chasing bad guys with guns are activities you might want to avoid if you want to play it safe. But what if it was your job to do these things? You'd want to have the right safety equipment. Here are some inventions made to protect workers.

A hard-headed invention

Protecting heads is an old tradition. Soldiers have worn helmets in battle for thousands of years. But other kinds of workers need head protection, too. English coal miners may have been the first industrial workers to wear protective hats. They were strengthened with wire and stuffed with rags—primitive compared to today's hardhats. In 1929, American Edward Bullard patented a "safety hat" that looks very much like the hardhat coal miners, fire fighters, and construction and electrical workers wear today.

Safety on high

If someone asked you to dangle by a belt from the side of a building, would you do it? Would it help to know that window washers do it all the time?

Starting in the early 1900's, Clarence Rose worked on improving the safety belt for the workers at his window-cleaning company. Early belts for window washers often were connected to bolts attached to old window frames. The washer's feet rested on stirrups that hung from the window sills. These belts were not very safe.

Rose invented a much stronger belt system for the washer to sit in and safely "travel" on the job, too.

Bright idea

American Anna Connelly was one of many women who invented bridges, ladders, and alarms in response to a growing concern for fire safety in cities in the late 1800's.

Connelly's bridge, which included guardrails, stretched from a building to the one next door. This allowed people in the burning building to move across the bridge to safety.

An astronaut uses a Sky Genie.

Rescue safety

In 1960, the Los Angeles fire chief asked L. H. Himmelrich to develop a safe, simple device that would help fire fighters rescue people from high-rise buildings. Himmelrich's company developed "Sky Genie"—a device that would let rescuers lower themselves slowly on a nylon line. Sky Genie hooked to a rescuer's belt and let out the nylon line at a controlled speed. The Sky Genie could even catch a rescuer who started to fall. Later, the company developed a waist/chest harness to go along with Sky Genie. This harness made Sky Genie even safer.

Electrical workers, space program workers at the Kennedy Space Center, and forest service crews have used Sky Genies in high places, too.

Sprinkler head

Fire!

Where there's smoke, there's fire. And if a building has an automatic sprinkler system, there should be water, too.

The model for the first sprinkler system was developed about 1806. A main water pipe was connected to several pipes with holes in them. The main pipe's water valve was kept closed by a weight on a string. When a fire burned the string, the weights would drop and the valve would open, letting out the water. This system was never actually used, though.

Today's systems use heat sensors to open water valves at the right places. When the system turns on, an alarm is automatically sent to the fire department.

Bullet-resistant vest

Suit of armor

The vest of life

Picture the armor that knights in battle wore hundreds of years ago. The armor was clumsy and heavy, but it gave full protection. Today, police officers and other people who need protection in the streets wear bullet-resistant vests.

In the 1960's, a Canadian engineer named Jan V. Weinberger developed the special weave of nylon that is used in today's bullet-resistant vests. Several layers of this nylon can spread out the force of a bullet and weaken its impact.

Touchdown!

To professional football players, the game is serious work. In the early days, players had no helmets or pads. Many suffered serious injuries. Today's protective equipment helps make football safer. Shoulder pads are made of foam rubber. Tiny pockets of air cushion the game's blows. Some players have also begun to wear a new type of shoe with cleats set in a circle. These cleats don't catch in the grass when players *pivot* (turn quickly). This reduces ankle injuries.

Score six for safety!

INVENTIONS FOR

LEARNING

You've seen how people use inventions to have fun, to keep safe and healthy, and to get all kinds of everyday jobs done. But have you ever thought about how inventions help people learn about the world around them? In this chapter, you'll visit one of the world's first schools, meet the inventor of the telescope, and get acquainted with the tiny universe that can be seen only through a microscope. You'll also read about the special tools scientists use to explore the universe. So turn the page—and get ready to learn!

School Days
Sumerian Style

"Time to get up!" your mom or dad calls. Maybe the alarm clock is blaring, too. Where's your backpack? Remember there's a spelling test this afternoon. Do you need

to bring lunch today? Eat a good breakfast, get dressed in a flash, and you're out the door and off to—school, where else? Have you ever wondered who invented school?

No one knows who had the idea for school, or just when and where the first school opened its doors. It seems likely that some of the first ones were in the ancient kingdom of Sumer (SOO muhr), in what is now southeastern Iraq, about 5,000 years ago.

These early schools trained boys and perhaps a few girls to become *scribes*. In Sumer, scribes were the educated people who held the most important jobs. They learned to read and write in school. In those days, most people could not read or write, so scribes enjoyed great respect.

What was school like so long ago? Different! Some classes met in the teacher's home, which had a large courtyard in the center. Students sat in the courtyard on rugs while the teacher instructed them. These schools had no chalkboards. Instead, teachers wrote in the sand.

When and where

Historians believe that the pencil as we know it may have gotten its start during a violent rainstorm in England in 1564. The wind pulled up a huge tree, roots and all, and in the hole people found a great supply of graphite, a soft black mineral. People soon discovered that graphite could be used to mark paper. The first modern pencil—made of graphite glued inside a stick of wood—was made in the late 1700's.

The students also practiced writing. But they did not write the way you do today. Paper and pencils had not been invented yet. Instead, students used a rod-shaped tool called a *stylus* to make impressions in a tablet of damp clay. The end of the stylus was shaped like a wedge. Students wrote letters and words by using different combinations of these wedge-shaped impressions. This type of writing was called *cuneiform* (kyoo NEE uh fawrm).

Using the students' clay tablets, the teacher wrote out lists of words for them to copy. Then the teacher checked the

Tablet with cuneiform writing

results. As long as the clay stayed soft, the students could use the tablet over and over again by rolling it up and flattening out one side to write on.

Sumerian students worked hard. They went to school from sunrise to sunset. The teachers were very strict. Remember, these schools were mainly "invented" to train young people for the hard job of being a scribe.

Schools have changed a lot since then, of course. But in important ways they still are the same. Ancient Sumerian students studied some of the same subjects you do. They learned about the world around them, and they studied mathematics, language, and perhaps drawing. But today, there are so many more things to learn about. And you know what else? You have a lot more choices about what you want to be when you grow up!

New Eyes on Space: Galileo's Story

My name is Galileo (gal uh LAY oh), and I was born in a little Italian village called Pisa in 1564. Many people think I invented the telescope. Well, I did have many remarkable successes in astronomy. But inventing the telescope wasn't one of them. Here's the story.

In 1609, I heard about a marvelous new invention by a Dutchman named Hans Lippershey, who was a maker of eyeglasses. According to one story, two children playing in Lippershey's shop held up two lenses, one near the eye and the other at arm's length. They found that when they held the lenses a certain distance apart and looked through them, they could see faraway objects as though they were nearby. When Lippershey found out what the children had discovered, he mounted the lenses at opposite ends of a tube—and invented the telescope.

What's the word?

The word **telescope** comes from Greek words meaning "far away" and "to look." Other scientific terms that come from Greek words include **microscope** ("to look at small things") and **photograph** ("to write with light").

When I heard of Lippershey's invention, I decided to make my own. I understood that the lenses in a telescope worked by *refracting,* or bending, light rays. They gather light from faraway objects and focus it into an image that is *magnified,* or made larger.

My first telescope showed objects about three times larger than they appeared to the naked eye. I could see ships out in the sea two hours before they came into the harbor. I continued to work on making better telescopes until I had one that magnified about 30 times. And what an astonishing view of the world this gave me! I could clearly read the writing above a doorway a mile away.

On clear nights, I turned my telescope to the skies. What I saw took my breath away. Imagine how I felt to be the first person to see the surface of the moon close up. Everyone thought the moon was smooth and polished, like a great silver mirror. But I saw that it was rough and mountainous, and covered with craters. When I looked at the hazy band of light we call the Milky Way, I could see that it was made of stars. And when I looked at the planet Venus, I made one of my most important discoveries.

To the naked eye, Venus looks like a bright star. Unlike the stars, though, Venus moves across the sky from night to night. In my day, most people believed that the earth was the center of the universe and that all the planets, and even the sun, went around it. But I preferred the theory of a Polish astronomer named Copernicus (koh PUR nuh kuhs).

What's the word?

A **planet** is a heavenly body that circles the sun. Planets look like stars as they shine in the night sky. But unlike stars, planets move. Early skygazers noticed this. So they named these bodies after the Greek word *planetes*, which means "to wander."

When I pointed my telescope toward the planet Venus, I could see Copernicus' theory in action. Here's how:

Copernicus believed the earth and planets went around the sun.

I looked at Venus for many months. At first, it was a small, round disk.

Over time, its position and shape changed.

Slowly, as I watched from night to night, the disk darkened into a half circle.

At the same time, it grew bigger.

Soon, the half circle had changed into a slender crescent.

Finally, Venus seemed to disappear. But when it reappeared several days later, the same changes happened in reverse. First it was a crescent, then a half circle, then a full glowing disk once again.

What was happening? I realized that Venus was not going around the earth at all. It was going around the sun. Venus was reflecting light from the sun, just as the moon does. As Venus moved in its orbit, I could see less of this light because the planet was between the earth and the sun. It was also getting closer to the earth, which explained why it looked bigger. I had seen with my own two eyes that Copernicus was right. Planets, including the earth, orbited the sun.

I published my findings. Was I hailed as a great discoverer? Absolutely not! Did you know that sometimes scientists and inventors can be "ahead of their time?" In my lifetime, many powerful people thought my ideas were dangerous. They believed the earth was the center of the universe— and that was that. I was forced to deny my beliefs in public, and I lived out my old age in loneliness, living in a world not ready to accept the truth.

FAR HORIZONS

The Keck Telescope

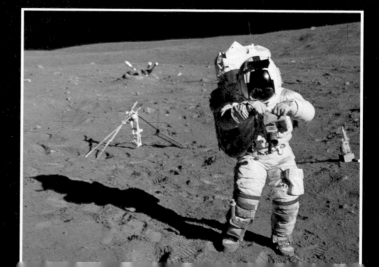

An astronaut
walking on
the moon

Jupiter

Think about how much we've learned about our universe. Astronauts have walked on the moon and brought back rocks to study. Probes have flown past, orbited, or landed on every planet in the solar system except Pluto. On earth, telescopes have peered into the reaches of faraway galaxies. They have helped us study such outer space mysteries as *black holes,* which are collapsed stars with gravity so strong that not even light can escape from them. Still, we have barely begun to explore the universe.

What are some new inventions that will help us learn more about our universe? Today, scientists are building giant telescopes to study distant stars and galaxies. The world's largest *optical* telescope (telescope that works with light) is the Keck Telescope in Hawaii. It was completed in 1992 and is 33 feet (10 meters) across.

But even bigger telescopes are in the works. Why is bigger better? The bigger a telescope is, the more light it can gather from objects in outer space. The more light, the better pictures it can provide.

What's the word?

A **satellite** is an object that circles a planet or other object in space. The moon is a natural satellite. A satellite that people have made is called an **artificial satellite.** On October 4, 1957, the Soviet Union launched *Sputnik,* the first artificial satellite to orbit the earth.

4.6-billion-year-old moon rock

The Hubble
Space Telescope

But no matter how big a telescope is, the view of outer space from earth is limited. This is because the *atmosphere* (AT muh sfeer), or layer of air around the earth, blurs the view. The way to get clearer pictures from telescopes is to put them in outer space, where there is no atmosphere. In 1990, the United States launched the Hubble Space Telescope. It has beamed back many fine pictures of distant objects in space, even though its mirror is flawed.

But telescopes can only show pictures of the universe. To learn more, we have to travel to space ourselves.

Space stations are one way to do this. Space stations are places where people live and work in space for weeks or months at a time. At a space station, astronauts can do scientific experiments and study the stars and planets. The Soviet Union launched the first space station, *Salyut*, in 1971. The United States followed with *Skylab* in 1973.

What does the future hold for people in space? Scientists are working on plans to set up a base on the moon, and

Skylab

This picture shows what a planned American space station, called Freedom, might look like.

to send astronauts to Mars. Nuclear-powered spacecraft that can travel farther on less fuel are also in the works. These craft may help make it possible to reach planets that are even farther away. Scientists are coming up with better ways to help people stay healthy on long space voyages, too. On spaceships of the future, greenhouses may supply fresh fruits and vegetables and special machines may recycle wastes.

Maybe someday we'll be able to visit some of the stars and galaxies that today we can only see through telescopes. We even may be able to travel to planets circling other stars—planets whose very existence we can only guess today. And with a whole universe out there, who knows what we'll find?

YOU CAN DO IT!

Growing food without soil

Things you need:

✓ empty glass jar
✓ cheesecloth
✓ rubber band
✓ alfalfa seeds*
✓ water

Space stations may grow food in unusual ways. Here's a simple activity you can do on earth—sprouting your own seeds without soil.

1. Sprinkle a single layer of seeds into the bottom of the jar.
2. Cover the seeds with water. Stretch a double layer of cheesecloth over the jar's top and hold it on with the rubber band. Soak the seeds overnight.
3. Drain the water out through the cheesecloth. Pound the jar to make the seeds fall back down or stick to the sides.
4. Let the jar sit for a few hours—not in direct sunlight.
5. Pour water in the jar again, through the cloth. Drain it out right away. Do this twice a day now, pounding your seeds down and still keeping the jar away from the sun.

6. Your seeds should begin to sprout in a day or two. When they're about an inch (2.5 cm) long, your sprouts are ready to eat. Toss them in a salad, or on a hamburger or sandwich for healthy eating.

*Alfalfa is a vegetable in the pea family. You can find the seeds at garden stores and health-food stores.

Human skin cells

Thinking Small

Would you ever have imagined that there is a whole universe of life in a drop of pond water? Or that every organ in your body is made up of tiny, living units called *cells?* No one did, until the invention of the microscope. No one is certain who invented the microscope. But it may be that the credit should go to Zacharias Janssen, a Dutch eyeglass-maker. About 1590, Janssen invented the principle of the *compound microscope.* This microscope uses two lenses—one to produce a magnified image of the object and another to magnify the image. Many microscopes still work this way today.

An English scientist named Robert Hooke also made a microscope, and used

What's the word?

There are some branches of science that depend on the microscope: **microbiology** (MY kroh by AHL uh jee): the study of microscopic living things; **entomology** (EHN tuh MAHL uh jee): the study of insects; **crystallography** (KRIHS tuh LAHG ruh fee): the study of the crystals that form many minerals and chemicals; **botany** (BAHT uh nee): the study of plants. Can you think of more?

Hooke's drawing
of cork cells

it to look at slices of cork. He saw thousands of tiny, empty chambers. These empty holes were places where cells in the bark of cork oak tree once lived. Hooke had discovered plant cells.

In the mid-1600's, Anton van Leeuwenhoek (LAY vuhn hook) became the first person to use the microscope to explore the unseen worlds far beyond the reach of the human eye. Leeuwenhoek, a Dutch amateur scientist, had great skill working with his hands, keen eyesight, and a good deal of patience. He needed all

Sometime between the years 1028 and 1038, an Arab scientist, Ibn Al-Haythan (IHB un ahl HAY thahn), also called Alhazen, wrote about light and vision. He was the first to study *refraction,* or the bending of light that causes magnification.

of these qualities to make the small lenses he used in his microscopes.

Unlike Janssen's compound microscope, Leeuwenhoek's microscopes had only one lens, like a tiny magnifying glass. He made hundreds of these single-lens microscopes. The most powerful of his microscopes that survive today magnified objects at least 270 times. (And the scientific observations he made show that he most certainly had more powerful microscopes, too.) When he looked at a drop of pond water, he saw tiny, moving objects. He realized that these must be living organisms. There were hundreds of thousands of them in one drop of water.

Some people did not believe that Leeuwenhoek's findings were real. They thought he was imagining the tiny creatures he saw through his microscope. But word of his discoveries spread, and other scientists began to see amazing things through their own microscopes. Suddenly there was a whole new universe to explore, as amazing as the one Galileo had seen with his telescope.

Leeuwenhoek put a drop of human blood under his single-lens microscope and discovered the tiny cells called *corpuscles* (KAWR puh suhlz), which carry oxygen to all parts of our bodies. He also

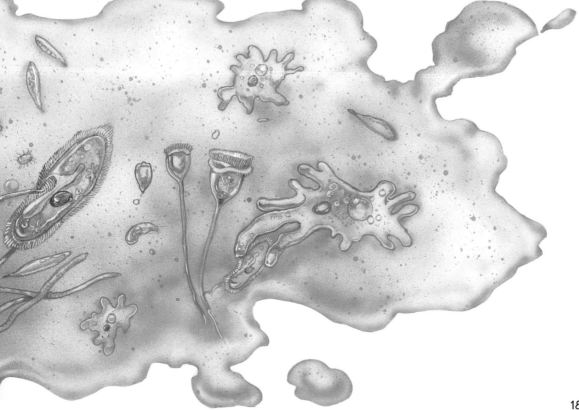

studied plants, examining the vessels that carry sap from one part of the plant to another.

As time went on, other scientists were able to improve the microscope. Because of their work, doctors learned about bacteria and *viruses,* the microscopic organisms that cause diseases. The microscope became a vital tool in the study of the human body and how it works.

In 1931, Ernst Ruska and other German scientists developed the electron microscope. This microscope can magnify objects up to 1 million times. It uses magnets to focus *electrons*—probably the smallest pieces of material that make up atoms—into a beam. The electron beam flows through whatever the microscope is examining, leaving a light and dark image of the tiny object. The magnified image then shows up on a screen.

An even more powerful microscope was invented in 1951 by a German-born American scientist, Erwin W. Müller. It is called the *ion microscope.* Müller

A researcher uses a compound microscope (above). Leeuwenhoek discovered red blood cells (above right).

continued to improve it until it could magnify samples of metal enough to show individual atoms.

With today's powerful microscopes, scientists hope to answer some of the most basic questions about matter and how it behaves. And this is not the end of the story. Microscopes continue to improve, allowing us to probe deeper into the world that is too small for our eyes alone to see.

What's the word?

Atoms are sometimes called the "building blocks" of matter. They are the smallest bits of a chemical element that still have the qualities of that element. An atom is made up of a mass of particles called *protons* and *neutrons* surrounded by electrons. All things—rocks, plants, water, even you—are made of atoms.

Electron scan of a tiny water animal called a *water bear*

Scientist using an electron microscope

INVENTING A NEW

WORLD

What will the future be like?

No one knows for sure. But lots of inventive changes are in the works. The world needs your ideas, too!

Inventions to help the environment are already at work, and more are being planned. With future inventions, people who can't hear, see, or walk might be able to do so, and cities may be cleaner and quieter. Scientists are developing ways to use plants to fight hunger and illness. And maybe someday we can live on Mars. Sound exciting? Go ahead and take a peek at the future. Just turn the page.

What's the word?

The English word **pollution** comes from the ancient Latin word for "impure." To pollute means "to make dirty." We use the word to describe the dumping of waste into the air and water and onto the land.

The Trials of

BILLY "BLUE BLOB" WATERS

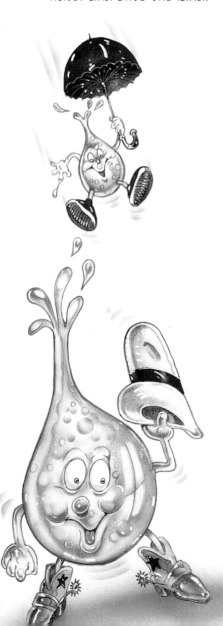

Howdy! The name's Billy "Blue Blob" Waters. I'm a sparklin' clean water drop.

Nothing riles me more than gettin' dirty. But some people can't seem to stop pollutin' us water drops. Just thinkin' about it makes me boil. Y'all can thank your lucky stars that folks have invented ways to clean up the water. Because without lots of clean water drops like me, your life would be mighty different.

You use more than 100 gallons (that's more than 380 of them liter things) of water every day. This used water is called *sewage*. And sewage is danged dirty.

Some people would rather just plunk sewage into the lakes and rivers. But mostly, people take better care of the water than that. Pipes usually carry the sewage from sinks, toilets, and bathtubs to water treatment plants—especially for you city folks. Machines at the plants screen out solid waste like hair and food scraps. Then the folks who operate the plants let helpful bacteria go to work removing harmful varmints that make water unsafe to swim in. They might add chemicals to purify the water and make it safe. And I'm sure glad they do—because Mama didn't raise her babies to be unsafe, no siree.

Folks are all fired up with new ways to clean sewage, too. I just heard that some inventors figured out a way to use a water plant called *duckweed* to clean water.

This here weed grows on the water and naturally "eats up" some kinds of sewage varmints. Clever, isn't it?

Sewage isn't my only problem, though. Another kind of water pollution comes from chemicals. Farmers use chemicals to help their crops grow and to kill weeds and bugs. Rain washes these chemicals into lakes and streams. Factories sometimes might dump or leak chemicals into the water. That makes me sore, you can bet. Lots of these chemicals harm animals and plants that live in the water. They aren't too healthy for people, either.

Of course, laws stoppin' this awful dumpin' have helped a heap. And so have laws stoppin' farmers from using bad chemicals. New inventions are in the works, too. I've even heard of one company that's raised a newfangled wormlike thing, called a *nematode*, that goes after the bugs that eat farmers' crops. The pesky bugs are wiped out without usin' bad chemicals, the crops look good, and the environment's still safe.

Chemicals are bad, but you wanna know what pollution I hate most? It's oil

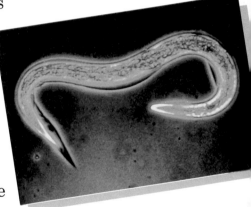

Duckweed

Nematode

American scientist John Todd invented a natural way to clean up sewage. Dirty water flows through sunlit tanks lined with microbes, algae, and plants. The microbes and algae feed on the sewage as it passes through the tank. Then they pass into other tanks, where they become food for larger creatures along the way.

spills. Boats called *tankers* ship oil all over the world. Sometimes, the tankers leak, or worse, sink. Oil in the ocean makes a mighty ugly mess. It also sticks to the food that birds, fish, and mammals eat. And when animals chow down on oil-coated grub, they get sick and die.

Scientists have learned how to grow critters called *microbes* that can live off oil. When there's an oil spill, workers might dump a mess of these microbes in it and they start eatin' the oil. When these critters have had their fill, they

Oil-eating microbes

usually become harmless fish food. After a nasty oil spill in Alaska back in 1989, scientists turned oil-eatin' microbes loose on the water to help clean it up.

Well, folks, before I mosey on down the pipe, I have one last thing to say to y'all—the best solution to water pollution is to keep water clean in the first place. In other words, you're darned tootin', you better stop pollutin'!

Energy for the Future

"**O**h no! The lights went out!" Has this ever happened in your house during a storm? If it has, they probably went back on pretty soon. Your parents didn't have to worry about food going bad in the refrigerator, and you were still able to watch your favorite TV show.

But what if the electric power didn't go back on? Then you'd really be in the dark, and in some ways life would be like it was more than a hundred years ago. Electrical energy, or power, makes life easier. In the future, it may be produced in ways that are cleaner and safer for the environment. What does this mean? Well, consider how we get our electricity now.

In the United States, we get most of our electricity from coal and nuclear power plants. Burning coal makes pollution. And nuclear power plants produce *radioactive wastes*. These very dangerous materials give off particles and rays that are harmful to people and all life.

Scientists are working to make these power sources cleaner and safer. Inventors are also turning back to "old-fashioned" energy sources and using them in ways that don't damage the environment. Take the sun and wind, for example.

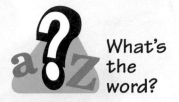

What's the word?

A **source** is the place from which you get something else. For example, coal, sunlight, and wind are all sources of electricity.

Cooling towers at a nuclear plant

This painting shows what a solar-powered spacecraft of the future may look like.

Wind turbines

Many devices, including solar collectors and solar cells, can be used to capture energy from the sun, called *solar energy*. The boxlike solar collectors trap heat that can be used to warm the air and water in a house. Solar cells can produce electricity. They are usually made from an element called *silicon* (SIHL uh kuhn). When light hits a solar cell, electrons in the silicon start to flow in an electric current. Many spacecraft are powered by electricity from solar cells.

Modern windmills, called *wind turbines*, use the force of the wind to turn blades on tall posts. The force of the turning blades powers a generator that produces electricity.

When and where

Farmers used early windmills to pump water out of the ground for their crops and animals. In 1890, a Danish inventor developed the first windmill that could generate electricity.

Some unusual "new-fashioned" sources of energy are appearing, too. In California, scientists are investigating ways to burn cattle manure to get energy. The burning manure produces steam that drives an electric generator. At one power plant, manure already provides enough fuel to bring electricity to 20,000 homes!

Other scientists are working with garbage in inventive ways. They have developed a way to generate electricity by burning the gases that are produced by rotting garbage in a landfill. If this catches on, your trash may someday be used to light your home. Then maybe you'll find yourself telling your children, "Please take out the garbage. We'll be needing the electricity."

When Dreams Come True

"Waiting for our parents at these meetings always takes so long," said Sara. "Want to play some basketball?"

"Sure," Al and Tom answered at once.

"Me too," said Nancy as she wheeled up to the group. Tom ran to get the ball.

"It must be a bummer not to be able to run around," Al said to Nancy.

"It's not so bad," Nancy smiled.

Sara chimed in, "Everyone tells me it must be hard not to see, but

I can do a lot of things that other kids can't."

"Like what?" asked Al.

"Like read with my fingers," Sara answered. "I know braille (brayl)."

"What's braille?" asked Nancy.

"Braille is writing made of raised dots. Each letter of the alphabet has a certain pattern. I run my fingers over the dots to read the letters and words. A young blind teacher in France, Louis Braille, invented the system back in the early 1800's, and we're still using it today."

"That's cool!" said Tom.

"And if a book isn't printed in braille," Sara continued, "there's a reading machine at the library downtown. It's a computer that can read to me. Or, it can reprint a story in braille so I can read it on my own."

"Neat," said Nancy.

"And scientists are inventing all sorts of things. Maybe someday they will invent artificial eyes that you could wear like glasses. They could send signals into your brain. Who knows? Maybe I'll really be able to see in the future. But even without all that, I can ski better than all my friends."

"You ski?" asked Al, wide-eyed.

Who did it?

Before braille was invented, Valentin Haüy of France taught blind people to read from raised letters. He wrote regular letters with a pen, pressing heavily so that the letters made ridges in the paper. Later, he invented a way to print raised letters and words on a printing machine.

What's the word?

The **Paralympics** are an international sporting competition for people with disabilities. It usually follows the Winter and Summer Olympic Games. The word *paralympics* comes from the words *paralyzed*—the loss of the ability to move a part of the body—and *Olympics*.

"Sure. I'd like to ski in the Paralympics when I get older," she answered.

"Well, I'm going to join a wheelchair track team when I get older," said Nancy. "And I'm planning to go hiking soon. Someday there may be wheelchairs that can climb steep hills and even go up mountains."

"Wow! A wheelchair that can climb mountains!" said Al.

"That's only half of it. For people who can't use their hands to work the controls on wheelchairs, there are wheelchairs that follow orders! You just tell the wheelchair where to go and it goes there. A French woman named Martine Kempf invented the voice-control part in

A wheelchair race at the 1992 Paralympics in Barcelona

the early 1980's. And soon, there even may be something I can wear on my legs like a pair of pants. The pants would walk for me, with the help of computers."

"It's really unbelievable what computers can do," said Al.

"My hearing aid has a computer in it already," said Tom.

"What does it do?" asked Sara.

"Without a hearing aid, I can hear some low voices and sounds, but I can't hear high ones. The computer is set to pick up the exact sounds I miss and make them louder—without making everything louder."

"A computer in your ear!" said Al.

When and where

Before electric hearing aids were invented, people who were hard of hearing used horn-shaped devices called "ear trumpets." The trumpets, which first appeared in the 1600's, helped funnel sounds into the ear.

Bright idea

Alexander Graham Bell, the Scottish-born inventor of the telephone, taught deaf children. He was always interested in ways to transmit sound to help hearing-impaired people. His father, Alexander Melville Bell, invented a code called "Visible Speech," a written system of symbols to help deaf people learn to speak.

"I still have trouble hearing on the phone, though. So I use a machine called a *TDD*—a telecommunication device for the deaf. All I have to do is type my message. The other person can read it on a screen on his or her TDD. Soon there will be machines that can hear what people say and print it on a computer screen— with no typing," said Tom.

"What about you, Al? Have any computers up your leg?"

"Not yet. But even so, I'm one of the better players on my Little League team. To think I never expected to run again

John Sabolich and Sarah East, the first youngster to use a Sense-of-Feel leg

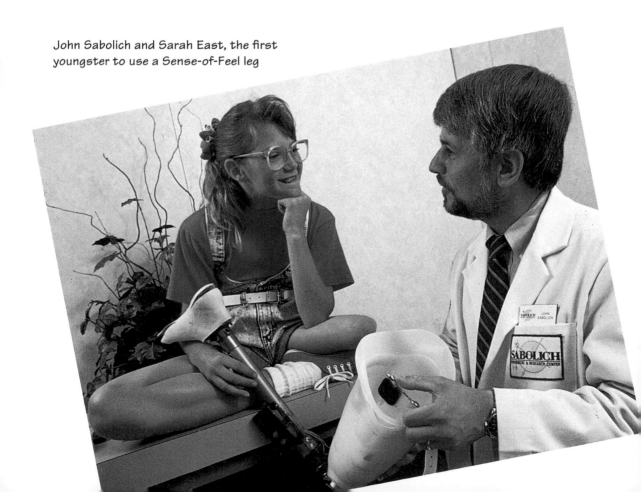

when I lost my leg. I still wish I could run without limping, though."

"Maybe you will," said Sara.

"I know. I've heard about an inventor named John Sabolich who's working on a 'Sense-of-Feel System' for artificial legs. His Sense-of-Feel leg has sensors that pick up the pressure of your foot against the ground. The sensors send electronic signals through wires up to your thigh. The leg gives you tingling feelings—it's like being able to feel your foot again. I hope I'll have one someday."

"We can keep up with other kids, any day!" said Tom.

"Yeah, and in the future we'll do even more!" said Sara.

"I can't wait!" said Nancy as she took aim with the basketball.

"She shoots. . . she scores!"

Scientists check on lettuce being grown without soil.

Plant a New Idea

Plants to the rescue! Did you know that plants can solve some of the world's problems? Read on. . . .

Relief from hunger and poverty

Imagine plants growing without soil. This kind of "almost instant" gardening takes place in Japan, where scientists are finding ways to grow vegetables quickly. In rooms controlled for temperature, light, and air quality, they grow plants by spraying nutrients onto plant roots. These nutrients help the plants grow faster. Lettuce that takes up to 90 days to grow in soil can be grown in about 30 days. People are hopeful that in the future some countries with drought or hunger problems can use this method to grow the food they need quickly.

Can plants be improved? Yes—and it's already being done with important food crops and other products that the world needs. Through genetic engineering, scientists take *genetic material*—that is, material in cells that is responsible for a living thing's features—from one plant and put it into another plant. The new plant

Genetically engineered plum tree seedlings

When and where

American scientists invented genetic engineering in the 1970's. The first patent for a genetically engineered plant—a new, more nutritious breed of corn—was issued in 1986.

A chemical in the bark of the willow tree is an ingredient in aspirin.

Who did it?

Charles Gerhardt, a French scientist, invented the first synthetic (human-made) aspirin in 1853.

is like the old one, but with the new feature added. Put these improved plants on the "genetically engineered" list: wheat plants that aren't harmed by a chemical used to kill weeds around them, tomato plants that won't rot if they're allowed to ripen on the vine before picking, and potato plants that release a poison that kills hungry insects but doesn't hurt people. In the future, farmers may grow more super healthful grains, vegetables, and fruits in any weather anywhere.

Medicine from plants

Did you know that aspirin has an ingredient that comes from the bark of a willow tree? People have used willow bark for centuries for treating fevers and headaches. Today, most drugs are made in laboratories, but many are based on natural materials found in plants.

Plants may be the key to the invention of many important medicines in the future. But researchers have tested less than ten per cent of the world's flowering plant species. One promising plant is the Pacific yew tree. Its bark contains a substance called taxol. Scientists are testing taxol for use in treating cancer.

When and where

For centuries, Native Americans used the bark of the South American cinchona (sihn KOH nuh) tree to make a medicine called quinine (KWY nyn). Quinine was used to treat malaria, a serious illness. Today, we have synthetic quinine, but natural quinine is still used to treat malaria in some places.

A scientist collects samples from the rain forest.

The Pacific yew contains a cancer-fighting chemical.

The background for this story shows what kenaf paper looks like.

Most of the untested plants grow in tropical rain forests. So some scientists and doctors are talking with people who live in the rain forests, hoping to learn how they use plants for healing.

Plants and the environment

Can plants be used in new ways to help the environment? Yes! Think of how much plastic you throw away every day. Plastics are hard to recycle. So scientists are working on genetically engineered plants that can replace some kinds of plastic. These new plants have fibers that are as strong as glass and can be treated so they don't absorb water. This fiber could replace plastic in many products.

Or what about using different plants to make paper? Today, almost all paper is made from trees, but inventors are studying the kenaf (kehn AF) plant as a new paper source. The kenaf plant grows in tropical areas and has strong fibers— the kind needed for papermaking. It's also fast-growing and can live in places where many trees can't. Scientists think this plant can save millions of trees.

Can you think of any other problems people face? Maybe a plant can help!

Bright idea

Today, most inks used to print newspapers are made from oil. Manufacturing these inks can be harmful to the environment. But in 1986, ink made from soybeans was used to print newspapers for the first time. Soybean ink comes in brighter colors, and it doesn't pollute!

Who did it?

George Washington Carver made more than 300 products from peanuts. Born a slave about 1864, Carver worked his way through high school, college, and graduate school. As an adult, he spent his life trying to improve crop production for struggling Southern farmers, many of whom were former slaves.

Through his research, Carver knew that cotton plants, the most common crop in the South at that time, used up minerals in the soil as they grew. Poor soil eventually led to poor cotton crops. Carver suggested that farmers plant peanut crops instead. Peanuts put minerals back into the soil. At first, farmers didn't like that idea. They didn't think they could sell enough peanuts to make money.

But Carver had his own ideas. He analyzed peanuts and reported that they were a very nutritious food. He also invented many uses for peanuts. The oils and proteins in peanuts were perfect for making margarine, ink, shaving cream, shampoo, and many other products. Because of Carver's research, peanut farmers earned good money, and the peanut became one of the most important crops in the South. It still is.

Welcome to My City

It's 2050, and this is the city where I live. Let me show you around.

Do you hear any traffic? Probably not. Cars are quiet now, and they run on electricity or solar-powered batteries. Those trains over there are actually moved by a magnetic force and float along a fixed track called a *guideway*. (Think about how the opposite ends of magnets repel each other.) These trains speed above the ground at hundreds of miles (kilometers) per hour.

Notice those tubes between buildings? They're sidewalks. We have underground sidewalks, too. They keep people out of bad weather and make the streets less crowded. And those glass boxes filled with people are "people-movers." They're a little like glass elevators that go sideways. They carry people to different places in the busiest downtown areas.

This is my favorite skyscraper. Its base is nine blocks wide. It has more than 1,000 floors and towers more than a mile (1.6 kilometers) into the clouds. In 1993, when my grandparents were young, the tallest building in the world—the Sears Tower in Chicago—had only 110 floors.

My city has its own forest. It was planted specially to release air-purifying oxygen through the tree leaves and provide shade. We also have our own city farm, where we grow a lot of the food that we sell in our stores. Would you like to live in a city like this? Maybe you will!

Bright idea

Tokyo, Japan, a city surrounded by water, is running out of room. One way to solve this problem might be "Aquatecture." It's a plan for floating greenhouses, factories, and transportation centers. The structure would make its own electricity from solar-, wind-, wave-, and thermal-energy sources. American students designed the Aquatecture plan for a Japanese contest and won first prize.

Living the Martian Life

The paintings in this story show how scientists think the settlement of Mars may begin. This painting shows what the first Mars landing might look like.

Far, far into the future, will some human beings be Martians? Before you think "no way," consider what some scientists have planned. Maybe, just maybe, your future relatives could live on Mars. Human beings have a pioneering spirit, and Mars has always fascinated people. The chance to start a new life on another planet would be irresistible for many people.

Scientists have already invented minirover robots here on earth to use for exploring Mars. Rovers could land on Mars before people arrived and pick up materials that could tell us about what the planet is made of.

We know quite a bit about this freezing, dry planet already. Its average temperature is -76° F. (-60° C). Earth has an average temperature of 59° F. (15° C). You won't find any lakes, oceans, or rain there. But before you think "so how could people live there, then?" consider what the two planets have in common. The soil and air on Mars share many of the same ingredients as the soil and air on earth. These ingredients include water (on Mars, it's frozen underground and at the north and south

What's the word?

A **Martian** would be someone who lived on Mars. We add the letters "ian" to certain "place words" to describe where someone is from. You could be a Californian, a Floridian, or a future Martian, for example. Using this rule, what might you be called if you lived on the moon?

Bright idea

American space scientists designed Rocky IV, the Mars "microrover." Rocky IV looks like a giant ant on six wheels. It has a mechanical arm with a pick and a scoop at the end for collecting rock and soil samples. It is lightweight since it is designed for travel, and—like many travelers—it carries a video camera.

poles) and chemical elements, including oxygen, which we need to breathe, and nitrogen, which plants need to grow.

Scientists think they can "stir up" these chemicals on Mars to make the planet more like the earth. If everything goes well, Mars could become so much like our planet that people could live there. Here's one way it might happen.

At first, Martian settlers would live in protected *biospheres* (BY uh sfeerz). Biospheres are large areas of land that are covered by domes. Under the domes, the air and temperature are carefully controlled.

Under a giant dome in Arizona called Biosphere II is a miniature world that includes ocean, desert, rain forest, and farmland. Researchers living in Biosphere II study how living things exist together. Their work may help people build a biosphere on Mars in the future.

Later, more scientists would arrive to build machines to warm up the air. The machines would take chemicals from the soil, change them, then pump them into the atmosphere. The new chemicals would "thicken" the air on Mars. The thicker air would trap more heat, and the planet would get warmer. How? Think of how a thick blanket keeps you warmer than a thin sheet.

When the temperature rose above freezing—at least 100 years later—the

frozen water underground and in the polar caps would start to melt. Water first would collect in small ponds and streams, and later turn into rushing rivers and large oceans.

When there was plenty of water on the Martian surface, scientists would grow plants. Early plants would be cold-loving plants like mosses and low shrubs. Trees need warmer temperatures than Mars would have at first. Then as Mars got warmer and warmer, scientists would add many other kinds of plants.

Live plants release oxygen into the atmosphere as they grow—the same chemical that people and animals need to breathe. As more and more plants grew on Mars, more and more oxygen would flow into the air. Factories could be built to add even more oxygen.

As the air became more like the air on the earth and the temperature continued to rise, people could start moving in. They could build houses, schools, and stores. The new Martians could enjoy meals of vegetables, fruits, and meats produced on Mars. They could swim in lakes and oceans and watch clouds in the sky. Living on Mars would be a lot like living on earth.

What's the word?

In 1952, a science-fiction writer, Jack Williamson, wrote about a character who invented machines to change the atmosphere on the moon so that people could live there. He called this process **terraforming** (Latin for "to make like the earth"). Today, scientists use this word to mean changing planets or moons to be more like the earth.

When could the project start? Some experts say in a hundred years or so, but it could be much later. Start-to-finish time would depend on what problems scientists run into along the way.

Does it all sound too far-fetched? Perhaps. And certainly not all scientists agree that we should try to change Mars. We would have to handle its environment very carefully to avoid damaging it. Watch for more news about this idea, and think about it yourself. You never know—there might be a whole new "world" out in space someday.

This painting shows what the first scientific base on Mars may look like. It includes a power plant, launch pad, living quarters, and greenhouses. At the front of the picture, an exploration vehicle climbs a hill while an astronaut collects rock samples.

Books to Read

Check at your school or public library for more books about inventors, inventions, and other discoveries that have changed our lives. Here are some titles you may enjoy.

Ages 5-8

✔ **Benjamin Franklin: Printer, Inventor, Statesman**
by David A. Adler (Holiday House, 1992)
Find out about the inventive life of this famous colonial American.

✔ **Eureka! It's an Airplane**
by Jeanne Bendick (Millbrook, 1992)
Follow the path of the invention of flying machines from gliders to rockets. You may also want to read **Eureka! It's an Automobile** by the same author.

✔ **My First Book of Time**
by Claire Llewellyn (Dorling Kindersley, 1992)
Early clocks and other time-measuring inventions are part of this beautifully illustrated book about time and how we keep track of it.

✔ **Samuel Todd's Book of Great Inventions**
by E. L. Konigsburg (Atheneum, 1991)
Follow witty young Samuel Todd around on a typical day and find out about basic, everyday inventions that make his life easier: Velcro, training wheels, his backpack, and his lunch-box thermos, among many others.

✔ **Voyager to the Planets**
by Necia H. Apfel (Clarion, 1991)
Find out about the building and operation of the *Voyager* spacecraft and follow the *Voyager 2* space probe on the journey that has taught us so much about the planets beyond earth.

Ages 8-12

✔ **Better Mousetraps: Product Improvements That Led to Success**
by Nathan Aaseng (Lerner, 1990)
This interesting book includes patent drawings and early photos and advertisements about products that we all know today. Also by the same author: **The Inventors: Nobel Prizes in Chemistry, Physics, and Medicine.**

✔ **Discovery and Inventions**
by Geoff Endacott (Viking, 1991)
A wide variety of inventions, from early printing technology and bridges to lasers and genetic engineering, are covered in this eye-catching book.

✓ **Galileo and the Universe**
by Steve Parker (HarperCollins, 1992)

Galileo's life and important work in science are covered in this well-written and illustrated biography.

✓ **Guess Again: More Weird & Wacky Inventions**
by Jim Murphy (Bradbury, 1986)

Have fun reading about all kinds of "weird and wacky" inventions and then trying to guess what they are. Information on patents and other more serious subjects is also included.

✓ **Invention**
by Lionel Bender (Knopf, 1991)

Printing, clocks, and computer chips are just a few important inventions covered in this book.

✓ **Inventions: An Amazing Investigation**
by Valerie Wyatt (Greey de Pencier, 1987)

This Canadian book is an entertaining account of inventions you can wear, eat, work, and play with. The author talks about "inventive thinking" that led to the inventions, too.

✓ **Mistakes That Worked**
by Charlotte F. Jones (Doubleday, 1991)

Was Coca-Cola really supposed to be a medicine? Find out about this and many other "inventive mistakes" that led to popular products.

✓ **Outward Dreams: Black Inventors and Their Inventions**
by Jim Haskins (Walker, 1991)

Both well-known and little-known African-American inventors are featured in this book, covering 300 years of American history.

✓ **The Story of Things**
by Kate Morgan (Walker, 1991)

"Things" are various important improvements in technology, such as the development of the wheel, that have made our work easier.

✓ **The Triumph of Discovery**
by Joan Dash (Messner, 1991)

This book tells about the lives and work of four modern women scientists—all Nobel Prize winners.

✓ **The Wright Brothers: How They Invented the Airplane**
by Russell Freedman (Holiday House, 1991)

Travel with *Flyer* as it finally gets off the ground. The pictures alone, which include many original photographs taken by Orville and Wilbur, make this book a fun and fascinating resource.

✓ **You Call That a Farm? Raising Leeches, Alligators, Weeds, and Other Unusual Things**
by Beryl Epstein and Sam Epstein (Farrar, Straus & Giroux, 1991)

Some farms raise shrimp that are used to test how toxic garbage is, or weeds that are used in making medicine. Find out how different and unusual farms can be!

New Words

Here are some words you have read in this book, mainly those that don't have a "What's the Word?" note in the margin. Some of them may be new to you. Next to each word you'll see how to say the word: synthesizer (SIHN thuh SY zuhr). Say the part in large capital letters louder than the rest of the word, and the part in small capital letters a little louder. One or two sentences tell the word's meaning as it is used in this book.

assembly line (ah SEHM blee lyn) A system of making a large number of products, such as cars, quickly. Workers make one part of a product and pass the product along to another group of workers for the next step.

astrolabe (AS truh layb) An early instrument used for measuring the angle of a star or planet above the *horizon*—the place in the distance where sky and land seem to meet.

atmosphere (AT muh sfeer) The invisible mixture of gases around a planet. We often call the earth's atmosphere "air."

biosphere (BY uh sfeer) All parts of the earth—land, water, and atmosphere—where life is found.

biplane (BY playn) An airplane with two sets of wings, one above the other.

cell (sehl) The basic unit of matter making up all living things. Some living things have one cell. A person has 10 million million cells.

chip (chihp) A word often used to mean computer chip. A computer chip is a piece of the chemical silicon. It has pathways and switches that carry a computer's electrical signals and commands.

cuneiform (kyoo NEE uh fawrm) An early system of writing that was begun in the Middle East. Sumerian cuneiform had about 600 *characters,* which were marks that stood for words and syllables.

generate (JEHN ur ayt) To make or produce. Electric generators may produce electricity through the power of steam pressure or water pressure that runs a machine called a *turbine.* The turbine powers the generator.

glider (GLY duhr) An airplane with no motor. Gliders are held up by air pressure around their wings.

hourglass (OUR glas) An early timepiece that worked by emptying sand from one glass bulb to another, taking an hour.

lens (lehnz) A piece of curved, see-through material, usually glass or plastic. Lenses bend light to make objects appear larger or smaller than they really are. Lenses in eyeglasses bend light to sharpen blurred images.

microbe (MY krohb) A living thing that is so tiny it can be studied only when magnified with a microscope. Microbes include algae and bacteria.

Milky Way (MIHL kee way) One of billions of *galaxies*, or groups of stars, in the universe. The Milky Way includes our solar system, clouds of gas and dust, and hundreds of billions of stars.

mineral (MIHN ur uhl) A nonliving material found in nature. Atoms of minerals form crystal patterns and have the same chemical makeup wherever they're found. Gold, silver, diamonds, and quartz are examples of minerals.

nitrogen (NY truh juhn) A gas that makes up over three-fourths of the earth's atmosphere. Plants and animals need nitrogen to live.

nuclear (NOO klee uhr) Having to do with energy released by atoms. The *nucleus,* or core, of an atom may be split apart to release powerful heat and light. People can also use nuclear energy to produce electricity.

orbit (AWR biht) The path of an artificial satellite, moon, or planet around another object in space.

oxygen (AHK suh juhn) A chemical element, a gas, that is necessary for life. About one-fifth of our air is made up of oxygen.

particle (PAHR tuh kuhl) A tiny piece or bit. Three types of particles make up an atom: protons, neutrons, and electrons. Electrons have a negative electrical charge and whirl around a nucleus—a cluster of protons and neutrons.

pasteurization (PAS chuhr uh ZAY shuhn) A process of killing bacteria in food by heating it.

patent (PAT uhnt) A government paper that gives a person or a company the right to be the only one who can make or sell an invention. A patent gives legal protection against someone stealing an inventor's idea.

quartz (kwawrts) A mineral found in many rocks. A quartz crystal—a tiny piece of quartz with atoms arranged in a pattern—is used in electronic watches. A battery-powered computer chip makes the crystal vibrate to move the watch hands or show digital time.

radar (RAY dahr) A machine used to track the distance, direction, and speed of faraway objects, such as planes, ships, and satellites. Radar works by sending and receiving radio waves to and from the distant object.

radio waves (RAY dee oh wayvz) Invisible waves of energy that carry radar, radio, and television signals through the air.

radioactive (RAY dee oh AHK tihv) Having energy produced by the breaking up of atoms.

recycle (ree CY kuhl) To change or treat waste material so that it can be used again to make new products. Recycling cuts down on trash in landfills and the wasting of valuable resources.

refract (rih FRAHKT) To bend a ray of light with a lens.

seismograph (SYZ muh graf) An instrument for recording information about earthquakes and other movements of the earth's crust. A seismograph can tell where an earthquake is, how strong it is, and how long it lasts.

sewage (SOO ihj) Wastewater that comes from people's bathrooms and kitchens.

space probe (spays prohb) A rocket with scientific instruments that makes observations in space and sends information back to earth.

sundial (SUHN DY uhl) A round timepiece that shows daytime hours by casting a shadow on markers around a circle. A raised pointer in the dial's center creates the shadow.

synthesizer (SIHN thuh SY zuhr) A musical instrument that makes sounds electronically.

telescope (TEHL uh skohp) A device that uses lenses or mirrors in a tube to magnify distant objects, making them seem closer than they really are.

television signal (TEHL uh vihzh uhn SIHG nuhl) The pattern of energy carried through the air that makes sounds and pictures appear on a television set. A television camera creates a signal by changing light and sound into electronic signals.

toxic (TOHK sihk) Poisonous or bad for health.

water clock (WOHT uhr klahk) An early timepiece that measured the passing of hours according to the rate of speed that water flowed out of a container.

Illustration Acknowledgments

The publishers of *Childcraft* gratefully acknowledge the courtesy of the following illustrators, photographers, agencies, and organizations for illustrations in this volume. When all the illustrations for a sequence of pages are from a single source, the inclusive page numbers are given. Credits should be read from left to right, top to bottom, on their respective pages. All illustrations are the exclusive property of the publishers of *Childcraft* unless names are marked with an asterisk (*).

Cover: Aristocrat, Standard, and Discovery Bindings—Dennis Hockerman
   Heritage Binding—Carl Whiting; NASA*; Eileen Mueller Neill; Randy Verougstraete; Dennis Hockerman; Flax Art Supply Company*; Steven D. Mach; LEGO Systems, Inc.*; Jared D. Lee
1   Dennis Hockerman
2-3   Dennis Hockerman
4-5   Steven D. Mach
6-7   Randy Verougstraete; Steven D. Mach; Randy Verougstraete; Carl Whiting; Joe Van Severen; Eileen Mueller Neill
8-9   Steven D. Mach
10-11   Randy Verougstraete
12-13   Randy Verougstraete; Don Monroe*
14 15   Randy Verougstraete; National Eastern Monument*; Randy Verougstraete
16-19   Robert Byrd
20-21   Robert Byrd; Rube Goldberg, King Features Syndicate
22-23   Flax Art Supply Company*; Johnson & Johnson*; Johnson & Johnson*
24 29   Steven D. Mach
30-35   George Ulrich
36-37   Reale Library, Turin, Italy (SCALA)*; Royal Collection, Windsor Castle*
38-39   Royal Collection, Windsor Castle*; Ambrosiana Library, Milan*
40-41   Ambrosiana Library, Milan*
42-43   Steven D. Mach
44-45   Joan Holub; James Industries*
46-47   LEGO Systems, Inc.*; *World Book* photo
48-49   Joan Holub; Kransco*
50-55   Don Madden
56-57   *World Book* photo; Metropolitan Museum of Art*; Newark Museum, New Jersey*
58-59   © by Johnny Gruelle/© 1989 MacMillan, Inc./© 1992 Applause, Inc. All Rights Reserved*; Essex Institute, Salem, Mass. (Richard Merrill)*; Museum of Science and Industry, Chicago*
60-61   Mattel Toys*; Russ-Berrie*
62-65   Hal Just
66-67   Bicycle Museum of America, Chicago*; Hal Just
68-69   Randy Verougstraete; Culver*
70-71   RCA*
72-73   UPI/Bettmann; Randy Verougstraete
74-75   Steven D. Mach
76-77   Montgomery Ward & Company*; Lydia Halverson; Lydia Halverson; Lydia Halverson
78-79   Montgomery Ward & Company*; Lydia Halverson
80-81   Montgomery Ward & Company*; Lydia Halverson; Lydia Halverson
82-87   G. Brian Karas
88-89   G. Brian Karas; Kathleen Buck*
90-91   Geoff Dore, Tony Stone Images*
92-93   Eileen Mueller Neill
94-95   Strasbourg Museum, France*
96-97   Eileen Mueller Neill
98-99   *Childcraft* artwork by The Big Guy
100-101   Carl Whiting
102-103   Steven D. Mach
104-111   Eileen Mueller Neill
112-113   Eldon Doty
114-115   Eldon Doty; AP/Wide World*

116-117   Eldon Doty
118-119   Liz Callen
120-121   Bureau of the Census*; UPI/Bettmann*; Liz Callen
122-123   Liz Callen; Pulsar (*World Book* photo); Hank Morgan, Photo Researchers*; Brownie Harris, The Stock Market*; David Grossman, Photo Researchers*; Kid Works 2 (Davidson & Associates*)
124-125   Diane Paterson
126-127   Metropolitan Museum of Art*; George Suyeoka; *World Book* photo by Ralph Brunke
128-129   George Suyeoka; Richard Fickle; Diane Paterson
130-131   Steven D. Mach
132-133   Jared D. Lee; Western Reserve Historical Society*
134-135   Jared D. Lee; Kairos, Latin Stock/SPL from Photo Researchers*
136-137   Jared D. Lee; Bruno de Hogues, Tony Stone Images*
138-143   Carl Whiting
144-145   Bettmann; AP/Wide World*; AP/Wide World*
146-147   Robert Benson*; © The Nobel Foundation*; AP/Wide World*; © The Nobel Foundation*; G. Degrazia, Custom Medical*; UPI/Bettmann*; Pfizer Inc.*
148-149   Steven D. Mach
150-151   Paul Chesley, Tony Stone Images*
152-153   National Oceanic and Atmospheric Administration*; U.S. Geological Survey*
154-155   George Ulrich
156-157   NASA*; Factory Mutual Engineering Corporation*; Western Reserve Historical Society*
158-159   Greg E. Mathieson*; Renee Lynn, Photo Researchers*
160-161   Steven D. Mach
162-163   Eileen Mueller Neill
164-165   Eileen Mueller Neill; Oriental Institute, University of Chicago*
166-171   Jared D. Lee
172-173   Roger Ressmeyer, Starlight*; NASA*; NASA*; NASA*
174-175   NASA*
176-177   NASA*; Eileen Mueller Neill
178-179   Joe Van Severen; Mike Peres, Custom Medical*; Joe Van Severen
180-181   Joe Van Severen
182-183   Terry Wild; Custom Medical*; Robert Schuster/SPL from Photo Researchers*; National Institutes of Health*
184-185   Steven D. Mach
186-187   Joe Van Severen
188-189   Harold Hungerford, Tom Stack and Assoc.*; Biosys Systems*; Joe Van Severen
190-191   Joe Van Severen; © Pasteur Institute/CNRI, Phototake*
192-193   Paul Meisel; Carol Lee, Tony Stone Images*
194-195   NASA*; © Tony Freeman*; Paul Meisel
196-197   Joe Van Severen
198-199   Joe Van Severen; Gray Mortimore, Allsport*
200 201   Sabolich Research Center; Joe Van Severen
202-203   NASA*; Agricultural Research Service, U.S. Department of Agriculture*
204-205   Pamela J. Harper*; Dan Stultz; Missouri Botanical Garden*; Michael Ellis*
206-207   Brown Bros.*; Paul Ristau
208-209   Paul Ristau
210-211   NASA*; NASA*
212-213   NASA*; © Tom Lamb, Space Biospheres Ventures
214-215   NASA*; NASA*
216-217   Steven D. Mach
218-223   Jared D. Lee

Index

This index is an alphabetical list of the important topics covered in this book. It will help you find information given in both words and pictures. To help you understand what an entry means, there is sometimes a helping word in parentheses, for example, *ENIAC* (computer). If there is information in both words and pictures, you will see the words *with pictures* after the page number. If there is only a picture, you will see the word *picture* after the page number.

Property of Calvin Wiley School